HIDDEN ASSETS

HIDDEN ASSETS
Harnessing the Power of Informal Networks

By Charles Ehin

Westminster College of Salt Lake City, Utah

Kluwer Academic Publishers
Boston/Dordrecht/London

Distributors for North, Central and South America:
Kluwer Academic Publishers
101 Philip Drive
Assinippi Park
Norwell, Massachusetts 02061 USA
Telephone (781) 871-6600
Fax (781) 681-9045
E-Mail <kluwer@wkap.com>
Distributors for all other countries:
Kluwer Academic Publishers Group
Post Office Box 17
3300 AH Dordrecht, THE NETHERLANDS
Tel: +31 (0) 78 657 60 00
Fax: +31 (0) 78 657 64 74

E-Mail <services@wkap.nl>

 Electronic Services <http://www.wkap.nl>

Hidden Assets:
  Harnessing the power of Informal Networks
  By Charles Ehin
      p.cm.
  Includes bibliographical references and index.
  ISBN 1-4020-8081-6 (alk.paper)
  E-ISBN 1-4020-8082-4

Permission for books published in Europe: permissions@wkap.nl
Permissions for books published in the United States of America: permissions@wkap.com
Printed on acid-free paper.
Printed in the United States of America

The Publisher offers discounts on this book for course use and bulk purchases. For further information, send email to <kluwer@wkap.com> .

Dedication

To Betty, my life's companion.

Contents

Preface

The purpose of this book is to shed light on the seldom "explicitly" accessed interactive triad of organizational success factors—self-organization, social capital, and tacit knowledge--from an in-depth human nature perspective. I believe that once people grasp the fact that individuals and groups are constantly self-organizing and that the process can't be strictly controlled, they will be able to design enterprises that are able to support the formation and functioning of these emergent systems *unobtrusively*. Knowing how to access and leverage these powerful forces will give any organization a much greater prospect to succeed in the turbulent Knowledge Age global landscape.

More precisely, *Hidden Assets* presents a clear and comprehensive system for increasing an organization's capacity for generating intellectual capital (or new knowledge) and for maximizing overall "voluntary" collaboration. Clearly, only the spawning of increased levels of innovation will provide companies in industrialized nations a competitive edge in the future since low wages, not only of blue-collar employees but also of highly educated and skilled personnel, in less developed countries are forcing businesses to take their work off-shore at an ever accelerating pace.

Certainly, businesses have become less bureaucratic in the last few decades. However, the efforts made to "empower" individuals and teams at all levels of organizations, to say the least, has been dismal. Central to the problem is the lack of models other than the standard prototypes for command-and-control systems. Unfortunately, the generation of knowledge is particularly dependent on voluntary collaboration and self-determination, foreign to the Industrial Age management mind-set that still plagues us.

Consequently, companies presently have no *comprehensive models* to follow for implementing "truly democratic" or self-organizing systems needed to increase the innovative capacity, productivity and commitment of knowledge workers. I believe I have developed precisely such a fundamental template which focuses on the informal or emergent social networks where, ironically, most of the work in organizations is accomplished in the first place.

The foundation for the book is "relatively" simple and straightforward. Being a long time interdisciplinary thinker helped me to put the pieces of the puzzle together with the help of the latest research findings in various fields such as anthropology, evolutionary psychology/biology, molecular biology, neurosciences, paleontology, and management. If I was a management "purist," I don't believe I could have put together the fundamental framework for this work.

Hence, I was intrigued by the fact no one had looked at emergent networks/groups other than from a relatively traditional perspective. That is, much has been learned about the "informal organization" but little has been done, other than the design of various social network analysis instruments and software applications in trying to leverage the tremendous power (I estimate that at least 70% of the work in organizations is accomplished by voluntary self-forming interactive groups) of these informal networks.

In the past decade attempts have been made to use the above mentioned devices in business. Regrettably, they are being employed to identify and *manage* these casual social arrangements. As one might deduce, that is an oxymoron. How do you manage an informal entity? It is an impossible (and undesirable) task. Once one begins to manage or control something it ceases to be informal. Such systems can only be *unmanaged.*

Essentially what I have done is to pinpoint and show the dynamic relationships of three primary factors that are the foundation of informal systems present in all social groups including businesses. These interdependent factors are comprised of self-organization, social capital, and tacit knowledge. Each of these factors has been separately written about previously, but no one has shown the synergistic power that can emanate from the interplay of the forces within this triad.

The catalysts for the interactive events among the triad of organizational success factors in my proposed system are the genetic- and experience-based elements encompassing human nature. Few people to date have "dared" to factor in genetics when developing models for organizational change and renewal. The reasons for that reluctance are clear-cut. The deep-seated characteristics of genes affecting human behavior were not well understood at the turn of the last century. As a result, false deterministic evolutionary concepts like Social Darwinism and Eugenics were espoused and eventually taken to the extreme by the Nazis.

The knowledge of certain basic features of our genetic tendencies can help us develop organizational contexts that *openly* support emergent systems instead of pushing the continuously evolving informal networks underground. Such an accommodating framework will allow the power and synergy of the triad to be fully accessed.

Accordingly, with an array of interrelated models, I demonstrate how such an organizational context, I call a *shared-access system,* can be developed. As expected, the core of a shared-access system is comprised of the voluntarily unleashed energy of the triad or "hidden wealth."

Acknowledgments

My wife, Betty, provided invaluable help in doing the initial editing and proofreading of the manuscript. She made sure that the work was "readable" from a common sense point of view and she was always there to give me plenty of encouragement and tender loving care during my moments of despair. My daughter, Linda Sampson, lent a hand in the proofreading and editing of the manuscript and did the preliminary design for the cover. Linda also provided helpful advice from a practical perspective.

Three other individuals made valuable contributions in the writing of this book. My friend and long time colleague at Westminster College of Salt Lake City, Professor Ken Meland, assured that the manuscript "passed the mustard" from both a theoretical and practical perspective. He also pointed out that my work had essentially filled the gap between management concepts based on the "visible" organizational elements such as structure, rewards, strategy, etc. and the assortment of motivational theories requiring leaders to have a deep psychological awareness of each individual in order to motivate them to their best effort.

Another friend and young entrepreneur, Mike Matheson, whose mind I apparently didn't "impair" irreparably while he was completing his MBA at Westminster College, provided several very sensible suggestions to make the work more understandable and readable. In addition, my long time friend and seasoned business expert, Carl Champagne, constantly offered his advice as I was developing my models and made sure that everything made sense from a day-to-day business standpoint. As a computer engineer, he was also always there whenever I needed technical support. Carl was especially helpful when I was compiling the final version of the manuscript for publication.

Finally, Sean Lorre and the entire staff at Kluwer Academic Publishers were extremely supportive from the moment my work was accepted for publication. It was an extreme pleasure to work with a world class organization and people that didn't cut any corners and were always there to help me throughout the publication process and beyond.

Chapter 1

INTRODUCTION
Discounting Human Nature

Most individuals will probably agree that adaptive self-organizing systems (systems that manage themselves without an imposed hierarchy or designated control mechanism) are best for dealing with a constantly changing information rich environment. However, what the majority of people still fail to grasp is that all living systems, including humans, have evolved to function independently in a self-organizing mode 24 hours a day, seven days a week.[1] Harder yet to fathom is the fact that even people in prisons, gulags, concentration camps and very tightly run top down organizations continuously self-organize in response to the demands of their immediate surroundings and conditions.

1. IGNORING A FUNDAMENTAL FACT OF LIFE

Well-seasoned folks have intuitively understood this fact for millennia. The "formal" discovery, though, that people self-organize all the time had to wait until the Hawthorne Studies were conducted at the Western Electric Company in the late 1920s and early 1930s.[2] The discovery was labeled the "informal organization" and was said to be unavoidable and uncontrollable in any social entity. It was also pointed out that these emergent systems may or may not pursue the goals formally established by an organization.

The critical question is, "If the informal organization or self-organization is a fact of life, then why isn't it one of the major topics for discussion in our executive suites?" Ignoring it certainly is illogical. If self-organization is unavoidable, then doesn't it make more sense to try to take advantage of the phenomenon and its associated dynamic factors instead of doing the impossible by trying to circumvent it or unsuspectingly pushing it underground? It's a fact of life (and all of us have experienced it in our places of work) that emergent informal groups, rather than people strictly complying with official policies and directives, accomplish most work in our institutions. Therefore, these evolving networks represent nearly all of the human potential of any social entity. What is most regrettable is that this "invisible wealth" remains largely untapped because it's a hidden resource that can't be tracked in the traditional sense nor is it included on any financial statements. That's a tremendous waste of human energy and novel ideas.

In the past five decades much has been learned about networks. There is now even a growing academic field called the "science of networks" that has become quite interdisciplinary in its makeup. In fact, some of the sociologists participating in this new field have developed an instrument called social network analysis and software applications such as Spoke and Visible Path that make it easier to pinpoint and diagram specific categories of informal networks within social systems.[3] As a result, efforts are currently under way to use these tools in business. Unfortunately, these experiments in industry are being employed to identify and manipulate or "manage" these casual social arrangements.

As one might surmise, that is an oxymoron. How do you manage an informal entity? It's an impossible and, for that matter, an undesirable undertaking. Once one begins to manage or control such systems they cease to be informal and serendipitously transform themselves. Thus, informal networks can't be managed in the traditional sense. Rather, the tremendous power of emergent systems can only be enhanced and amplified by a supportive organizational environment.

The well known network scientist, Duncan J. Watts, suggests that:

Although we still don't fully understand the problem, it appears that a good strategy for building organizations that are capable of solving complex problems is to train individuals to react to ambiguity by searching through their social networks, rather than forcing them to build and contribute to centrally designed problem-solving tools and databases. The big payoff of this approach is that by understanding how individuals search socially, we can hope to design more effective procedures by which robust organizations can be constructed without having to specify the precise details of the organizational architecture itself.[4]

In Hidden Assets I do precisely what Watts suggests is required for "the big payoff." I propose organizational contexts and procedures from an evolutionary, biological, and neurological perspective necessary for accessing the hidden yet powerful assets lurking below the surface of every organization.

So, whether we like to admit it or not, all activities and interactions between people are governed by the principles of self-organization. Consequently, we need to learn what some of the essential principles of self-organization and human nature are in order to draw on this powerful but invisible resource present in all our social institutions. Essentially, our goal should be to develop organizations where we practice unmanagement (a term I coined at an Academy of Management Conference in San Jose, California in 1995) on the people side and manage the inanimate "stuff." That seems to be the most practical approach.

2. FOUR ESSENTIAL FACTORS

In the future smart organizations will recognize the criticality of the following four general factors and organize their efforts accordingly:
1. Knowledge and knowledge professionals can't be managed in the traditional sense.
2. All life forms are self-organizing systems by design, down to their individual cells and molecules.
3. All biological systems have genetically transmitted behavioral tendencies modified by their life experiences for responding to different environmental conditions.
4. The more an institution supports the principles of self-organization *openly,* the more social capital and tacit knowledge it will generate which, in turn, will lead to increased levels of innovation and entrepreneurship.

Understanding self-organizing principles is especially important when dealing with knowledge professionals. The reason for that is quite simple. The generation of knowledge is an indiscernible voluntary cooperative process as opposed to a practice where the movement of hands and feet can be observed as was/is the case with the industrial workforce. New ideas can't be forced out of people because they seldom know exactly what knowledge they possess.[5] Recent research also shows that a threatening environment, by creating negative emotions, narrows thought patterns by necessity. Conversely, positive emotions enhance more expansive and resourceful thinking essential for creativity.[6]

Further, all life forms, including humans, have one common purpose for existence and for self-organizing all their efforts around this zeal no matter what conditions they may encounter. Specifically, that innate purpose is to survive long enough to perpetuate the species by passing on the genes to the next generation.[7] Interestingly, survival of the fittest isn't the primary mode to accomplish that common purpose. Rather, mutual accommodation among and within species and chance are the major forces that impact survival. We're also not born with a blank slate for a mind. Instead, we arrive with all the rudiments of our mental circuitry in place ready to act in response to our immediate surroundings and, at the same time, we are able to learn from our experiences.[8] Thus, we are equipped not only with instincts, but also with much broader innate drives or predisposed genetic tendencies such as concern for status and for affiliation. This means that our behavior is influenced by our genes rather than genetically determined and that we do have free will.[9] As Steven Pinker so succinctly stipulates in *The Blank Slate: The Modern Denial of Human Nature*, "human nature is the problem, and human nature is the solution."[10]

Finally, it seems paradoxical but I submit that the more an institution is openly governed by self-organization or unmanagement the more essential social capital it will generate. The rationale for that is straightforward. Social capital is generated and maintained by voluntary interdependent personal connections that are mutually supportive. That, of course, is the foundation for self-organization. Such an environment also facilitates the emergence of tacit knowledge—the wellspring of all new knowledge. Thus, the hidden riches of any social system consist of a powerful triad of interdependent but invisible dynamics—self-organization, social capital, and tacit knowledge.

3.   PURPOSE OF THE BOOK

The purpose of this book is to shed light on this seldom "explicitly" accessed triad of organizational success factors. Once people grasp the fact that individuals and groups are constantly self-organizing and that the process can't be strictly controlled, they will be able to design enterprises that are able to support the formation and functioning of these emergent systems unobtrusively. Knowing how to access and leverage these powerful forces will give any organization a much greater prospect to succeed in the turbulent global landscape.

Essentially, Hidden Assets presents a clear and comprehensive system for increasing an organization's capacity for generating intellectual capital (or new knowledge) and for maximizing overall "voluntary" collaboration. Clearly, only the spawning of increased levels of innovation and entrepreneurship will provide companies in industrialized nations a competitive edge in the future since low wages not only of blue-collar employees but also of highly educated and skilled personnel in less developed countries are forcing businesses to take their work off-shore at an ever accelerating pace.

The foundation for the book is "relatively" simple and straight forward. Being a long time interdisciplinary thinker helped me to put the pieces of the puzzle together with the help of the latest research findings in various fields such as anthropology, evolutionary psychology/biology, molecular biology, neurosciences, paleontology and, of course, management. If I was a business or management "purist," I don't believe I could have put together the fundamental framework for this work.

Hence, I was intrigued by the fact no one had looked at emergent or informal networks/groups other than from a traditional perspective. That is, much has been learned about the "informal organization" (that they are always present for good or for bad) but little has been done, other than the design of the social network analysis instrument, in trying to leverage the tremendous power (at least 70% of the work in organizations is accomplished by these "invisible" groups) of these informal networks.

Consequently, in Hidden Assets I show how to fill the gap between management concepts based on the "observable" organizational elements such as structure, rewards, strategy, et cetera and the assortment of motivational theories requiring leaders to have a deep psychological awareness of each individual in order to motivate them to their best effort. Institutions that will make a serious effort to access their hidden human potential will not only be more productive in their endeavors but also more human friendly. After all, the interdependent triad of organizational success factors isn't just about running social institutions but about life itself.

What I have written isn't an academic study but rather a practical guide for any social entity or individual wanting to prosper in today's Knowledge Age. Clearly, I have had to incorporate certain theoretical aspects into the work from the latest research in multiple fields. That, of course, needed to be done to strengthen and make more explicit the overall practical framework of the book. I'm convinced that fostering the indiscernible dynamics of informal networks will be the key to success of any social entity in the years to come.

4.   THE JOURNEY

Chapter Two provides a general overview of the importance for closing the gap between management concepts based on the "observable" organizational elements and the assortment of motivational theories currently being championed. Fundamentally, I demonstrate how most organizations fail to pay serious attention to the "gap" where ironically roughly seventy percent of the work is accomplished in all organizations.

Chapter Three is the longest chapter because it provides most of the scientific and theoretical background for the rest of the book. In it I reveal the most deep-seated principles for engaging people in exceptionally productive and truly collaborative efforts. In doing so, I first take a look back into our past to determine what the most successful and longitudinal method of adaptation has been in meeting the needs of social groups. That includes taking a close look at human genetic predispositions and the evolution of three primary modes for resource acquisition and distribution. Next, I explain why most of our organizations today are commonly run in a top down hierarchical rather than a democratic and self-organizing fashion. Finally, by comparing the current organizational methods to those of the distant past I propose new options for governing our social institutions more productively, creatively, and humanely.

The attention in Chapter Four is on understanding the difference between control and order. True, machines need to be externally controlled; however, all living systems innately seek order around them based on the conditions of their immediate surroundings. The myth of the Industrial Age that organizations must be structured and operated like machines has been so deeply ingrained in our minds that most people still have great difficulty in looking at social systems from a different perspective.

How to leverage the power of the invisible guiding hand, or self-organization, within an enterprise is the subject of Chapter Five. Ironically, there's nothing new or magical about the principles governing self-organizing systems. These universal rules have been supporting our kind for roughly 200,000 years and our close cousins for several million years before that. They have helped us to survive for 99 percent of our existence on this planet. I show why it is now high time that we focus on these principles openly instead of forcing them intentionally or mindlessly "underground."

In Chapter Six I describe the positive influence of shared or "no bossing" leadership in achieving and maintaining high levels of organizational commitment instead of relying principally on member compliance. In the past, and still to a considerable degree today, people have mistaken position power with leadership. Hence, I show why position power seldom equates to real leadership and that true leadership is about encouraging others to pursue mutually beneficial goals rather than attempting to control them.

The focus of Chapter Seven is on how an organization can more consistently recognize the best possible options to pursue when faced with endless opportunities and problems appearing on the horizon. I also illustrate the criticality of environmental scanning, real time feedback, and periodic "slack time" devoted to reflective thinking in enabling a self-organizing social system to attain its full potential. Without a relentless effort to exchange internal and external information, overt self-organization makes little sense.

In the final chapter I examine the remarkably close interdependent relationships between what I consider to be the three most decisive organizational success factors—informal self-organizing networks, social capital, and tacit knowledge. This invisible triad constitutes the untapped "wealth" of most social institutions worldwide. I also explain why simply satisfying the greed of knowledge workers or by further refining management methods of the past, organizations will not be able to reach their full potential in years to come.

Chapter 2

HIDDEN ASSETS

Have you ever wondered how things actually get accomplished in most organizations *despite* all the obstacles continuously encountered by the people who perform the day-to-day activities? I'm sure you have unless, of course, you are one of those rare individuals who is independently wealthy and who has never worked for someone else their entire life. Unsurprisingly, all of us also have our own individual theories why businesses survive in spite of the seemingly unworkable systems and processes they frequently employ.

Just in case you may have, for a moment, forgotten what those obstacles are let me list just a few of the most common ones in order to make sure we're all on the same page. I seriously doubt that anyone has failed to encounter at least some of the following problems:

- Unclear goals and objectives
- Ambiguous or unexplained policies and procedures
- Unrealistic deadlines and budgets
- Pressure to do more with less
- Lack of cooperation and teamwork
- Poor and uninspiring leadership
- Lack of open communications and trust

Can you imagine what the net gains would be in wealth, creativity and social responsibility that could be realized by enterprises that discovered how to leverage the hidden but powerful attributes that allow firms to make a profit in spite of the barriers mentioned above? I suggest that the possibilities are boundless. Also, mergers and change initiatives in general would be much more successful than studies show today.

At present we are firmly immersed in a knowledge economy. Hence, harnessing the talents, skills and commitment of knowledge workers (now more than a third of the US workforce[1]) is the most fundamental challenge for business of our time. Just imagine the additional wealth that could be generated if the creative abilities of the rest of the workforce were also unleashed. Regrettably, however, most corporations (consciously or unknowingly) still insist on using the industrial model developed and refined during the past three centuries.

Certainly, businesses have become less bureaucratic in the last few decades. However, the efforts made to "empower" individuals and teams at all levels of organizations, to say the least, has been dismal. By and large, most members of firms remain disenfranchised. Thus, unsurprisingly, workers (especially knowledge workers) feel alienated from their organizations thereby causing their efforts to be limited by distrust and cynicism.

Central to the problem is the lack of models other than the standard prototypes for command-and-control systems. Unfortunately, the generation of knowledge is particularly dependent on voluntary collaboration and self-determination, foreign to the Industrial Age management mind-set. Consequently, companies still have no *comprehensive* working models to follow for implementing "truly democratic" or self-organizing systems (not to be confused with the assortment of "flat" hierarchies currently being promoted) needed to increase the productivity and commitment of knowledge professionals or, for that matter, workers in general.

I believe I have developed precisely such a fundamental template. As a result, in *Hidden Assets* my focus is on informal or emergent social networks where, ironically, most of the work in organizations is accomplished in the first place. These invisible self-organizing systems are present in all social entities. For that reason, I've designed an all-inclusive framework that includes an array of integrated models showing how to "support" (as opposed to manage) these informal networks so that they will voluntarily unleash their tremendous energy and creativity in support of the formal goals and objectives of an enterprise.

Further, information technology and its by-product, the virtual organization, are indispensable tools for success in today's information rich and rapidly changing environment. They provide the means for instant exchange of explicit knowledge around the world. However, these tools alone are of limited value for supporting the development of social capital and "quarrying" the tacit or undiscovered knowledge residing within every individual and informal group of an enterprise.

Accordingly, organizations and individuals that want to prosper in the Knowledge Age must soon realize that commitment (as opposed to compliance) and the sharing of ideas are dependent on the extraordinarily delicate *balanced interface* between the invisible dynamics of human nature enhanced by the appropriate use of information technology. Understanding how living systems function in response to their immediate environments will allow organizations to "mine" and leverage the hidden wealth that has been ignored for so long.

1. MISSING THE MOTHER LODE

My principal center of attention is on demonstrating the remarkably close mutually supporting relationships between what I consider to be the three most decisive organizational success factors—*informal self-organizing networks, social capital, and tacit knowledge.* These emergent processes, instead of people strictly complying with official policies and directives, are the foundation for most work performed in our institutions. I estimate that the triad of unseen success factors is responsible for roughly two thirds of the effectiveness of any venture. Regrettably, these powerful invisible forces are not even partially tapped by most of our organizations.[2] Thus, they consistently keep missing "the mother lode."

For example, researchers have studied the concept of organizational "absorptive capability" (ACAP) for over a decade now.[3] ACAP is defined "as a set of organizational routines and processes by which firms acquire, assimilate, transform, and exploit knowledge to produce a dynamic organizational capability."[4] *Social integration methods* are a key component of ACAP yet, to my knowledge, no serious effort has been made to demonstrate to what extent self-organization, social capital, and tacit knowledge impact the process.

Figure 2-1 depicts "the gap" between the visible organizational components and recognized motivational schemes. In effect, ignoring or not knowing how to *leverage* (as opposed to control or manage) the three interdependent emergent forces creates a "choke point" hindering the possibility of attaining full benefits from the modifications made in the other two elements. That is precisely why most mergers and organizational change efforts fail to produce the desired outcomes in the long run. This will become progressively clearer with each succeeding chapter.

Figure 2-1. Filling the Gap

What we continue to overlook is that humans (and all other living entities) have evolved to function quite well independently without superimposed structures and motivational systems. If that was not true our kind could not have survived as a species as long as we have. Thus, it is high time that we also begin to grasp and leverage the innate powers of human nature in our organizations instead of continuing to almost exclusively rely on top down control processes which at best generate compliance rather than commitment. It's a costly neglect.

What is also not commonly known is that the dynamics of invisible emergent systems represents most of the human potential of any social entity. As a result, because the triad of organizational success factors is an imperceptible resource that can't be tracked in the traditional sense (it isn't included in any official financial statements) it remains largely untapped. Hence, it's not surprising that studies continue to validate that about 80 percent of all mergers fail to create the expected benefits anticipated[5], that most change efforts fall short of their targets; that some individuals can perform at 20 to 30 percent of their ability without losing their jobs; and that the average employee works only at two-thirds of his or her capacity.[6]

That is a tremendous waste of human energy and novel ideas. Therefore, in the chapters that follow, I provide the most comprehensive and practical framework to date for the development of "smart" organizations that can benefit from the invisible power and knowledge embedded within every enterprise. More than 70 years ago we "formally" identified the existence of emergent systems in our social institutions. It's now high time that we put that knowledge to practical use.

The most productive applications of my theoretical framework apply to organizations primarily dependent on new innovative products and services. The general principles, however, are applicable to any social system. Nevertheless, new possibilities require new ways of thinking. Unfortunately, old mind sets and philosophies persist long after they are productive. New ways of thinking don't just happen; they require new models which have to be learned and applied by visionary first adopters who, of course, also reap the highest returns in the long run.

My aim is to help people grasp the importance of understanding and applying the fundamental survival principles of living entities that can't be circumvented no matter how we try. Rather than attempting to dodge these unmanageable dynamics that are part of every social entity or push them underground, we need to learn how to cultivate them openly. That's the only way we can realistically quarry the invisible wealth of organizations. *More notably, self-organization, social capital, and tacit knowledge is not just about running private and public organizations but it is also about the very foundation of life itself.*

2.   THE TRIAD

Fundamentally, what I have done is to pinpoint and show the *dynamic relationships* of three primary factors that are the foundation of informal systems present in all social groups including businesses. As suggested before, these *interdependent* factors are:
- Self-organization
- Social capital
- Tacit knowledge

Each of these factors has been separately written about previously, but no one has shown the synergistic power that can emanate from the balanced interplay of the forces within this triad.

For example, multidisciplinary research has confirmed that all biological organisms, including humans, function in a self-organizing mode internally and externally. That is, our bodies, down to individual cells and DNA molecules, work together in order to sustain us, but there is no central "boss" to control this dynamic activity. Our relationships with other individuals also progress through the same circular free flowing process as we search for outcomes that are best for our well-being. Under the right conditions these social exchanges can be extraordinarily altruistic. Conversely, they can also be quite self-centered and even violent. It all depends on the immediate environment and the people involved.

Further, within a company the self-organizing process leads to the development of social capital or the goodwill available to individuals and groups. Social capital is generated and maintained by the voluntary structures and the contents of peoples' relationships. Its effects flow from the information, influence, and solidarity it makes available to the informal network participants. High levels of social capital make it possible for an organization to accomplish extraordinary feats without the need to acquire added resources.

Finally, tacit knowledge, the wellspring of all new knowledge, is something we all possess (otherwise we couldn't survive for a day), but we really can't delineate explicitly until we are faced with a specific problem or opportunity. Hence, when a person or group is confronted with an unusual event, tacit knowledge begins to emerge serendipitously resulting in the development of a fitting response (explicit knowledge) to the episode. Clearly, tacit knowledge can't be managed or forced out of people since it's a constantly evolving ephemeral domain. Thus, its emergence can be best supported by voluntary cooperation.

3.   THE CATALYSTS

The catalysts for the interactive events among the triad of organizational success factors in my proposed system are the genetic- and experience-based elements encompassing human nature. Few people to date have "dared" to factor in genetics when developing models for organizational change and renewal. The reasons for that reluctance are clear-cut. The deep-seated characteristics of genes affecting human behavior were not well understood at the turn of the last century. As a result, false deterministic evolutionary concepts like Social Darwinism and Eugenics were espoused and eventually taken to the extreme by the Nazis.

Fortunately recent research in molecular biology, neurology, and the Human Genome Project are helping to eradicate past and present evolutionary fabrications. Thus, at least in the scientific community, it's now widely accepted that our genes do *influence* behavior but that these influences hardly equate to genetic determinism. In essence, I've taken the fundamentals of human nature to the next level by suggesting how to make practical use of its building blocks in our social systems.

For instance, the knowledge of certain basic features of our genetic tendencies can help us develop organizational contexts that *openly* support emergent systems instead of pushing the continuously evolving informal networks underground. Such an accommodating framework will allow the power and synergy of the triad to be fully accessed. Accordingly, with the aid of an array of original interrelated models, I demonstrate how such an organizational context, I call a *shared-access system,* can be developed. As expected, the core of a shared-access system is comprised of the voluntarily unleashed energy of the triad or "hidden assets."

What I developed is not a prescriptive system where one size fits all because that's an impossible task when dealing with diverse groups of people. Every organization is unique in its make-up and operation. Rather, what I have created is a broad integrated framework founded on the latest research from multiple scientific fields. The principles I have delineated and integrated are grounded in common sense (which, unfortunately, is seldom very common) and practicality. Although I don't ignore information technology (IT) and its importance, my focus is primarily on self-organizing processes governed by *unmanagement* that must be well cultivated and appropriately supported before IT can be put to effective use.

4. FUNDAMENTAL CONSIDERATIONS

Four fundamental issues need to be kept in mind in our quest for increased commitment, creativity, innovation, and productivity in our organizations based on the principles of unmanagement. I'll explain these factors in more detail in the chapters that follow. First, we must realize that knowledge is classified into two categories: explicit and tacit.[7] You may want to refer to Figure 7-2 for a graphic representation of the dynamic interrelationships between the two types of knowledge.

Explicit knowledge is any information that has been formally defined and codified. Thus, it is usually gained through sources such as formal education, training, books, and the Internet. *Explicit knowledge is a static resource.* That is to say, it does not contain the capacity to renew itself. An outside entity needs to keep it current.

Tacit knowledge, on the other hand, encompasses ideas and abstractions at the individual level. It's acquired by life experiences and by interacting or working with more experienced people. There is also a physiological reason why tacit knowledge differs from explicit knowledge. Very simply, "...different brain systems are involved in implicit forms of memory, on the one hand, and conscious/explicit/declarative memory, on the other."[8] I'll discuss this more in Chapter Six.

Unrelated or unexpressed knowledge comes to the fore serendipitously as individuals or small groups confront new or unanticipated situations. Consequently, *tacit knowledge is a dynamic resource.* Hence, although relatively stable, implicit knowledge continues to be shaped by our continuous interactions with our immediate surroundings and other people. Most importantly, unconnected know-how is the wellspring for all new knowledge.

Clearly, there is a circular cause-and-effect relationship between the two categories of knowledge. Explicit knowledge (a specific event or a newly published theory) triggers fresh ideas (tacit knowledge), which then leads to the development of more codified information that can be applied productively. Thus, implicit knowledge must first be made explicit before it can be put to practical use.

It's important to remember that tacit knowledge must be allowed to *emerge* through voluntary collaboration or self-organization. It can't be forced or managed out of individuals since people seldom are aware of exactly what unrelated knowledge they possess until confronted with a problem or an opportunity where they perceive themselves to be a key participant.

Therefore, in order for tacit knowledge to be able to properly emerge, people must first be surrounded by a supportive environment. Threats, for example, create negative emotions that, by necessity, narrow thought patterns.[9] People threatened by the loss of their jobs, a bullying boss, not knowing what their status is from day-to-day and so on innately narrows their thought patterns to avoid or eliminate these negative emotions first. As a result, such individuals unconsciously devote little or no time to engage their minds more expansively and resourcefully in search of new ideas.

This leads us to the second essential issue for enhancing productivity and knowledge generation—human nature. Without thoroughly understanding who we are as biological systems there is little hope of developing a well functioning learning organization. Unfortunately, for roughly the past century, our focus has been almost exclusively on the purely psychological aspects of human nature. That is, we have been primarily concerned with how the environment molds our neurological framework as if our brains are a blank slate when we are born. Hence, we have almost completely ignored, until very recently, the biological or genetically transmitted side of our mental response systems.

The latest scientific evidence shows quite convincingly that it is a fifty-fifty proposition between our genes and the environment in forming our personalities and modes of behavior. Therefore, we are not born with a blank slate for a mind to be completely shaped by our surroundings, but rather we come equipped with certain predisposed tendencies, which are expressed or not expressed (also strengthened or atrophied by constant employment or non-use) depending on our immediate environmental context. Clearly, our experiences have an affect on our behavioral tendencies but so do our genes. What must be thoroughly understood is that the most recent research does not support the notion of genetic determinism. Rather, it suggests that our behavior is *genetically influenced* and that we do have free will.[10]

If we use a multi-story building as an example of our neurological system, then we have until very recently concentrated almost our entire focus on the middle floors to the penthouse. It is now time that we pay attention to the entire building from the basement up in designing and running our organized efforts. James Watson, President of Cold Spring Harbor Laboratory, has made it quite clear where we are headed genetically as far as psychology is concerned. According Watson:

> The next century will bring together biology and psychology. In the past, I never wanted to learn psychology because I didn't think its proponents had a solid basis for what they claimed. Now we're going to begin to understand behavior from a genetic perspective.[11]

In essence, we should begin to appreciate the significance of the invisible guiding hand (self-organization) in our day-to-day activities and interactions.

Fundamentally, we are born with two basic categories of innate drives (genetic predispositions that are considerably less reactive than pure instincts), a set of *self-centered drives* (e.g., concern for control, rank, status, territory, possessions) and a set of *other-centered drives* (e.g., concern for attachments, affiliation, altruism, care-giving, care-receiving). Humans function best in an environment where they are able to express both categories of drives in a balanced manner.[12] That will be clarified in Chapters Three and Five.

Unsuspectingly, most of today's organizations, with their prevailing top-down management systems, are mainly impacting their people's self-centered drives as they seek out their best discernible *individual* survival alternatives. Simultaneously, their leaders are asking these individuals to be good team players and deeply committed to the goals of the enterprise. Obviously, this is not an effective way to run knowledge based institutions where the development of social capital and the exchange of tacit knowledge is the key to success and, therefore, the other-centered drives also need to have an opportunity to be expressed.

We are born with the capacity to anticipate and to respond to changes in our immediate environment in addition to learning from our experiences. So, whether we like to admit it or not all activities and interactions between people are governed by the principles of self-organization. Therefore, we need to learn what some of the essential principles of self-organization and human nature are in order to draw on this powerful but invisible resource present in all our social institutions.

At this juncture you may want to take a moment to reflect on your own experiences in relation to the invisible triad of organizational success factors alluded to above by beginning to search for answers to the following questions: "How often have you accomplished something noteworthy and creative that made a very positive impact in your place of work by strictly following official policies and procedures?" "Why did you 'voluntarily' seek the counsel or aid of certain individuals/groups and not of others while working on a memorable project?" "What were some of the creative and innovative ideas that 'emerged' in your collaborative efforts?"

The third critical factor in developing knowledge-intensive enterprises is size. There is now ample evidence that human beings are physiologically incapable of developing and maintaining mutually beneficial *voluntary* collaborative relationships within groups larger than 150 people.[13] In larger collectives, relationships become fragmented, ties of common interest cannot be properly sustained, and hierarchical structures begin to creep in.

Consequently, from a human nature perspective, small size is absolutely essential for the development of positive environmental contexts where informal groups and networks can flourish *openly*. What this also implies is that *capitalism without a strong sense of community ultimately can lead to unrestrained greed* as exemplified by the Enrons and WorldComs. Humans are not fundamentally "noble savages" nor are they uncompromisingly self-indulgent. We are capable of both extremes given the appropriate surroundings. By no means, however, do I mean to imply that large institutions can't benefit from the dynamics of small groups. I will expand on this point later in the book.

Finally, what we also need to set aside are the two persistent myths about pecking orders or organizational chains of command. Hierarchies are necessary in certain situations but they are not appropriate for all social endeavors. The problem with a hierarchy is that it is founded on two false assertions that also serve as the foundation for its advocacy. The first premise suggests that hierarchies are an unavoidable phenomenon among humans. This argument is true only if we prefer to rely primarily on the most primitive drives of the lowest level of our three-tiered brain—the reptilian complex that evolved almost 500 million years ago.[14] If we believe that humans are more intelligent than reptiles, it would make more sense (at least occasionally) to rely on our characteristically human social side, especially with respect to creativity and innovation.

The second contention supporting the hierarchical model is grounded in the belief that social organizations should be structured in accordance with a mechanistic or machine metaphor. That is, organizations should be developed and run like well-oiled machines. Engineers and economists initiated this philosophy during the Industrial Revolution. The problem with this premise is that it confuses control with order. People are not machines by any stretch of the imagination. Machines need to have external control mechanisms. People naturally self-organize around any situation or opportunity, thus establishing situation-specific order.

What are the implications of what we have covered so far? The four fundamental issues outlined above suggest that the Knowledge Age demands that we understand what drives us and learn not to waste time and money trying to circumvent human nature. By understanding our inherent genetic predispositions and how the environment affects them, we can begin to leverage the tremendous power that resides in the invisible parts of every organization. Without recognizing the vitality of the hidden social dynamics, organizations will continue to curb their capabilities in the years to come. *We need to recognize that life by and large is good when one pursues things that are good for life in general.*

Chapter 3

UNDERSTANDING WHO WE ARE

Today one of the most pressing questions that needs to be answered is, "Why can't knowledge workers be *managed* in the traditional sense?" I suggest that the answer to this question is firmly grounded in our insights regarding human nature. Hence, this chapter explores in detail who we are and makes explicit certain key organizational principles that we need to adhere to in the information rich decades ahead.

In the Industrial Age (and still today in many instances) people were primarily hired for the use of their hands and feet instead of their minds. The thinking and directing was the job of the bosses. Essentially, organizations were designed and run like machines. As a result, employees were treated as expendable interchangeable parts and costs of production.

Conversely, workers needed various forms of equipment and tools that these organizations possessed in order to make a living. In other words, they had to have access to "means of production" since, with rare exceptions, they couldn't afford to acquire their own machines and facilities necessary for the attainment of sufficient wealth for adequate subsistence.

Knowledge professionals of today, who constitute more than a third of the United States workforce (and their numbers are constantly increasing), are faced with a completely different yet subtle situation. What is subtle is that they own their means of production—the gray matter between their ears. Consequently, when they decide to join or leave an organization they carry their means of production with them.

Knowledge workers are an investment and, therefore, require not special attention but balanced treatment so they will not walk out the door permanently. Interestingly, giving them more money and other benefits will not have the desired effect in the long run (I will explain this in Chapter Seven). Tacit knowledge simply can't be forced or "bribed" out of people.

Knowledge professionals not only desire considerable personal autonomy but also the responsibility and accountability for running at least some part of an organization. Thus, they need to be treated as partners or associates not as typical Industrial Age employees. That in a nut shell is the reason why knowledge workers can't be managed in the traditional sense. But there is much more we should understand about knowledge generation and the knowledge worker. In essence, we need to develop organizations that continually nurture the collaborative best from all members and, in turn, reward them equitably and not just from a monetary standpoint.

To be able to realistically accomplish that feat we must first take a look back into our past in order to understand who we really are and to determine what the most successful longitudinal methods of adaptation have been in meeting human societal needs. Next, we need to understand why most of our organizations today are run in a top down hierarchical fashion. Finally, by comparing the two states, we can begin to envision more realistic organizational options that we may want to pursue in the future. However, before we begin to examine our past social arrangements it is crucial that we first understand what the common purpose of all living systems is and what role "survival of the fittest" plays in our quest for relevant organizational frameworks.

1.   LIFE'S COMMON PURPOSE

All life forms, including humans, have one common purpose for existence and for self-organizing all their efforts around that zeal no matter what conditions may be encountered. That purpose is *to survive long enough successfully to perpetuate the species and (depending on the species) pass on the accumulated knowledge/culture to the next generation.* Interestingly, survival of the fittest is only part of the mode to accomplish that purpose. So, let us take a closer look at this seldom discussed but basic fact of life and its importance in running our organizations.

Most people have little difficulty in agreeing that surviving long enough to pass on our genes to the next generation is the most "basic" reason for our existence. However, they usually immediately qualify their responses by stipulating that genes are responsible only for the purely biological side of our existence but not the mental aspects of our makeup. Namely, that the intellectual characteristics of an individual are primarily acquired though learning and life experiences. That may be a noble thought but it's only *partially* based on reality.

Before our ability to scan an active brain it was difficult to convince people that the psychological aspects of our makeup were not separated from the biological side. Technology has now made that argument quite mute, although many among us still have difficulty in accepting this fact.[1] As Seven Pinker stipulates, "...when it comes to the question of what makes people within the mainstream of a society different from one another— whether they are smarter or duller, nicer or nastier, bolder or shyer—the nature-nurture debate, as it has been played out for millennia, really is over, or ought to be."[2] Most of the scientific community now agrees that roughly fifty percent of people's personalities are molded by genes and the other half by life experiences. Further, from an evolutionary perspective, we know that behavior evolved first and the ability to make sense of it developed later.[3]

Very simply, disassociating our psychological framework from the biological is impossible and contrary to all the latest scientific evidence. They are inseparable, since the basis for our needs and behavior reside in the expression of our genetic makeup. That is to say, everything we do both physically and mentally is accomplished through the expression of our genes.[4] Denial of that simple fact will only hinder the development of organizational frameworks that are best suited for the needs of the Knowledge Age and for people in general. This is the very reason that there are no "chiefs" or control mechanisms in our bodies, including the brain. Every part of our bodies, down to the individual molecules, works *together* in a self-organizing manner because there is no doubt what the common purpose is, both in thoughts and deeds.

We constantly seek novelty and pleasure in order to improve our survival capabilities as well as those of our kin and close friends. Consequently, our creative talents, including our abilities to make an impression on people around us and in turn to be influenced by the gifts of others, are part of our survival repertoire. The expression of these innate drives makes life meaningful, motivating us to pursue increasingly higher initiatives and goals. Art, for instance, can be considered to be the by-product of three adaptations: "...the hunger for status, the aesthetic pleasure of experiencing adaptive objects and environments, and the ability to design artifacts to achieve desired ends. Whether art is an adoption or a by-product or a mixture of the two, it is deeply rooted in our mental faculties."[5] I will explain the influences of our genetic predispositions in more detail later in the chapter.

2.   NOT NECESSARILY SURVIVAL OF THE FITTEST

Another important aspect of our evolutionary past needs illumination in conjunction with the discussion of life's common purpose—the concept of survival of the fittest. True, new life forms evolve and certain others gradually disappear. However, the latest scientific evidence clearly indicates that survival of the fittest isn't the only basis for evolution or for survival in general.

What the experts say is that self-organization and random chance have much greater impact on evolution than survival of the fittest.[6] Theoretically, if survival of the fittest was the primary process for evolution, then all life would have vanished from our planet a long time ago leaving the last life form "standing meritoriously in the ring" all by itself.

To begin with, biological systems are not continuously evolving towards greater complexity.[7] There is no master plan. Evolution is like a bush that grows in stages. Branches grow from the trunk and, in turn, other branches grow from the branches. Thus, a given species evolves and remains stable for a considerable period in which little change takes place. It may then sprout a new but similar species (branch or branches) and then eventually disappear.

Modern humans (Homo sapiens), for example, have not changed much anatomically in roughly the past 200,000[8] years (the estimates range from 100,000 to 400,000 years). Hence, our mental and physical capacities have altered inconsequentially since the dawn of our species. As the noted biochemist Charles Pasternak has stated:

> The potential of man to write and to draw, to analyse and to construct, to oppress and humiliate, was there 100,000 years ago. We were as clever and as vindictive then as we are today. All that has occurred—especially rapidly in the last 10,000 years—is an accretion of accomplishments.[9]

What this means is that knowledge is accumulative and that we're not much more intelligent now than we were a couple hundred thousand years ago in coping with our surroundings. Our recent record speaks for itself. Only our technology, cultures and environment have changed. That is precisely why we need to be very cognizant of not widening the gap between our unchanging human nature and the new social and technological contexts, which we have largely imposed on ourselves. We can literally be our own worst enemies.

Survival of any life form depends more on serendipitous and symbiotic relationships (self-organization) and chance than completely on competition. All one has to do to make sense of this is to visit a meadow or a forest and observe nature in action. There is no "CEO" directing the growth, activities and interactions among plants, insects and animals. Everything is interdependent and cooperation is accomplished without control. Only when we interfere and try to "manage" such systems do things go astray. The fact is that most mass extinctions of life on earth have been caused by random impacts of large comets and asteroids rather than "mortal combat" between species.

More than 300 million years ago our ancient forbearers competed (winner takes all) for food, territory and mates on an individual basis just as many vertebrates do today. About 100 million years later, as group living gained prominence and territory began to be shared, competition for *rank* (hierarchy) instead of territory became the principal mode for relationships within social entities. Nevertheless, the inborn need for every organism to assure its own well being didn't vanish with this new genetic predisposition, as is still the case today.

Higher rank brought with it better access to needed resources by having greater *resource holding power* (as opposed to winner takes all). Thus, competition by intimidation became the best option for survival. The down side to this form of existence is that the higher-ranking individuals keep members of a group at constant high levels of psychological tension through their "policing" actions, although physical outbreaks of aggression are minimized.[10] As one can readily deduce, most of our organizations today are still based on competition by rank or hierarchies.

In the last ten million years of evolution (and in a more accelerated fashion in the past two million years among primates and hominids as the growth of their brain sizes accelerated) a new form of competition emerged amid some species including modern humans and our immediate ancestors. Instead of competing by intimidating rivals it became more beneficial to attract them to collaborative mutually beneficial activities.

That is, attracting others with better hunting or foraging skill, a unique capacity for solving problems, and talent to entertain others (by song, dance or story telling) provides individuals *situation specific status* and with it greater access to needed resources. Today's classic examples of this phenomenon are famous entertainers, noted experts, and accomplished athletes.

What is especially important to remember is that this *social attention holding potential* is attained without coercion or position power but rather through expertise and self-organization. Further, status (as opposed to hierarchical power) gives individuals needed self-esteem and reduces psychological tension and violence within groups without the threat of punishment.

One can now see the importance of having high levels of self-esteem among organizational members especially when dealing with knowledge professionals and knowledge workers. How else can an organization achieve high-sustained levels of voluntary collaboration? Thus, concern for both status and affiliation are vital ingredients for a balanced work environment. I will discuss this in more detail in Chapter Five.

3.   ENDURING SOCIETAL SUCCESS FACTORS

In trying to determine what the most *enduring* societal survival mode was in the past 200,000 years or so of modern human existence and the reasons for its durability, it obviously makes little sense to use written history as the primary source for that information. Instead, the latest scientific findings in the fields of anthropology, evolutionary psychology, molecular biology, neurology, and paleontology need to be the foundations for the inquiry. In order not to be excruciatingly boring to the reader, I will only highlight the pertinent findings in these fields and suggest how the information can be put to practical use in today's environment in the ensuing chapters.

It may come as a big surprise to many people that modern humans have lived in small relatively egalitarian social groups for 99 percent of their existence.[11] Only fairly recently (about the past 15,000 to 20,000 years) have we again started to use rank and hierarchy as the primary means to run our social systems. How ironic. Eons ago our ancestors gradually began shedding "competition by intimidation" for "competition by attraction" and now millions of years later we are again expressing our more basic evolved genetic predispositions. No wonder our social problems are increasing.

So, what collective social form was the most successful and longitudinal adaptation modern humans have ever achieved? It was the immediate consumption (food was not stored and was consumed before spoilage) *hunting and gathering* way of life that originated in Africa and eventually spread to every continent. In fact, there is now evidence that our most recent ancestors, the hominids (several very human like shoots of the branch of life where we now reside alone), also had adopted the hunter-gatherer way of living several million years prior to modern humans.[12]

What is most pertinent about the hunter-gatherers is not *what* they did for their survival but *how* they conducted their day-to-day activities. That is, what were the fundamental success factors that governed the interactions of these social groups that might be equally relevant to today's knowledge organizations or any social institution for that matter? Modern "civilizations" certainly have yet to even come close to the longitudinal organizing feats of our ancient forbearers as is exemplified by the rise and fall of countless "advanced civilizations" in the past 10,000 years or so. For convenience, I will highlight significant organizing principles of the hunter-gatherers in the paragraphs that follow and then summarize their significance at the end of the section.

The best survival strategy for the hunter-gatherers, under conditions of uncertainty, variability of needed resources within a given region and high mobility, was to function in small very interdependent social groups of 30 to 50 people. Teams of three to four people did the actual hunting and gathering. Whole tribes seldom consisted of more than 150 members. These tightly knit, extended, kinship and friendship groups were also loosely linked to networks of similar small bands within a relatively large region.

As suggested above, these clans were extremely mobile, rarely staying in one location for more than one to four weeks, and traveled on foot about 1500 to 2500 miles a year. Also, reciprocity was a critical component of their lives. This was primarily due to the uncertainty of finding the necessary daily food sources to sustain the community. In fact, the custom of sharing was so strongly ingrained in their minds that *not* sharing food was never an option.[13] Of course, freeloading was not tolerated by the hunter-gatherers for obvious reasons and violators were severely punished.

There was obviously both a practical as well as a social reason for sharing food. On the pragmatic side, sharing took place for two reasons. First, food usually needed to be consumed within 48 hours before it spoiled. Second, daily hunting and gathering excursions, rarely lasting more than four hours, were carried out by several small teams of three to four people. The rest of the band stayed behind at the camp-site taking care of the children, making or repairing tools, resting and so on.

The social side of the ethic of sharing among the hunter-gatherers was just as significant. One must remember that these clans were composed of relatives and close friends. Thus, their reciprocity was also innately governed by life's common purpose—surviving long enough to perpetuate the species. Clearly, "Altruism toward strangers is a behavior not supported by natural selection."[14]

For example, in passing on the genes to future generations kin and *close* friends play a vital role. Relatives are also the carriers of an individual's genes. Therefore, if a specific person doesn't survive long enough to pass on his or her genes to the next generation then the relatives will still keep the lineage going. In addition, close friends are a key support element for both individual group members and their kin. They provide further assurance that the gene pool will be passed on to the future.

Hunter-gatherers didn't live in pure "communal" societies. First, clan members owned their own means of production similar to the knowledge workers of today. This included tools, weapons and other personal items. Only the fruits of the regional lands were collectively used and shared. Further, a high degree of individual autonomy existed. Band members were expected to be capable of being fully self-reliant in addition to having a strong sense for the importance of the success of the clan as a whole and the social ties that accompanied it. Thus, everyone was considered to be of equal intrinsic worth and capable of managing his or her own actions and relationships.

Interestingly, there were no status differences between men and women like there are today. Hunting and gathering were cooperative events and neither activity was considered to be more important than the other. Leadership was also fluid and situational or shared. Hence, both sexes assumed leadership roles depending on the circumstances and the expertise of the individuals involved. There were no chiefs to exert their position power and will over others. Decisions were made by consensus. The clans seem to have operated in a truly open self-organizing mode.[15]

It is also fascinating to note that our foraging ancestors consumed a very nutritious and balanced diet even by current standards. For instance, only from ten to twenty-five percent of their daily calories came from meat. The rest of the nutrition came from nuts, fruits, and various roots. As a matter of fact, there is now sufficient evidence that immediate-consumption hunter-gatherers were healthier and lived longer than later herders and farmers.

Further, research shows that the lives of modern humans for the first 99 percent of their existence were much less strenuous than is stereotypically portrayed, especially in old movies. Only a few hours a day, by only a fraction of the members of a clan, were dedicated to finding food. The rest of the available time was usually devoted to socializing, play, music, storytelling, and resting. It is also interesting to note that hunting as a game or sport was unheard of among our ancestors.

In particular, most of the free time of the hunter-gatherers was devoted to socializing. Even their transitory campsites were designed to maximize social interaction. For example, all of the entrances to the encircled, temporary shelters faced inward and the hearths were situated in front of the entrances. This configuration enhanced the continuous exchange of ideas and information no matter what the occasion was. Band members were always up to date on where they had all been, what had recently transpired, and what they intended to do next.

Finally, about every six weeks or so individual clans would reinforce and renew their social ties among the extended tribal network in the region. This was accomplished by the gathering of several of the independent groups for festivals that lasted for several days. Such large festive occasions were periods of intense social interaction including visiting, feasting, exchanging of gifts, and for finding mates.

One must remember, however, that our distant ancestors were not "noble savages," as some anthropologists have tried to portray them in the past, and that our kind has been "flawed" by the civilized world. That is to say, like us, they also could and did resort to violence (our most basic evolutionary survival mode) when that was perceived to be the most appropriate option. They were not saints by any stretch of the imagination.

4. INTERPRETING THE LONGITUDINAL SOCIETAL SUCCESS FACTORS

In summary, the critical success factors of our hunter-gatherer ancestors were:

- Lived in relatively small very interdependent groups composed of kin and close friends.
- Maintained high, sustained levels of reciprocity, egalitarianism, and practiced consensus decision-making.
- Clan members owned their own means of production.
- Respected individual autonomy and self-reliance tempered with social responsibility and accountability.
- Practiced situational or shared leadership based on expertise (social attention holding power) rather than rank (resource holding power) and there were no status differences between the sexes.

I will use the above critical success factors in Chapter Five to develop the four principles for supporting *overt* (as opposed to covert) self-organization. Now let's take a closer look at these factors and determine why they are important and how they might enhance the effectiveness of organizations today and in the future.

Lived in relatively small very interdependent groups. All the success factors are important because they work together reinforcing each other rather than contributing independently. However, small group size was by far the biggest contributor to the longitudinal success of the foraging societies.

Recall that roughly 300 million years ago our evolutionary ancestors fended for themselves independently. Later it became advantageous to exist in small hierarchical groups. Then about ten million years ago competition by attraction, rather than by intimidation, began to be used more and more in social groups. Finally, during the course of the last two million years the size of the brains among our closest mammal ancestors and ending with modern humans sprouted enormously.

For example, the human brain is nine times larger in relation to body size than that of mammals in general. Our closest primate relatives, the chimpanzees, have brains about six times larger than most mammals. Why did this sudden (relatively speaking) brain expansion take place? The latest evidence suggests that brains became larger not primarily for better tool making capabilities but also to support *social complexity*, which eventually led to the evolution of language.[16]   Fundamentally, larger mutually interdependent social clusters of people had a better chance to survive.

Research has revealed that mammals that maintain more complex social relationships have a larger neocortex (the upper brain that in humans constitutes about 75 to 80 percent of the brain mass) than those that do not. More importantly, the quality rather than the number of relationships maintained seems to be the main determining feature of the size of the neocortex.[17] In other words, "social creatures often need to exploit one another in the same way that nonsocial ones exploit food resources."[18]

Of course, the development of language has considerably expanded the capacity of humans to socialize. For instance, language permits us to speak to more than one person at a time. It allows us to exchange ideas, information, preferences, and other subtleties about ourselves and other individuals. In addition, language gives us the capability to talk about other people, allowing us to keep track of their behavior and relationships without having to constantly monitor them ourselves.

What is an extremely significant point to keep in mind is that our relatively large brains don't give us an unlimited capacity for social relationships. There is now ample evidence that the size of our neocortex restricts our voluntary collaborative social interaction to about 150 people. Not surprisingly, that was also the maximum size of a hunter-gatherer tribe.

Therefore, there is a limit as to how many individuals we can maintain *good intelligence* on. In groups larger than 150 people, relationships become fragmented, ties of common interest can't be effectively maintained, and hierarchies creep in. Essentially, within larger groups *overall* close social ties fade away becoming confined to small separate cliques and various formalized "control" systems slowly begin to take shape.

For example, if you've been part of a large organization you can easily recall the close casual relationships that you established within the confines of your immediate work environment. You may also have had informal ties to a few people physically located more distantly from your office or department. Fundamentally, however, most of the individuals in the company were simply a "number" to you no matter how much empathy you may have tried to have towards them.

One other critical aspect about group size needs to be brought to light. Small groups facilitate frequent face-to-face or line-of-sight interactions among its members. What is significant about face-to-face exchanges is that they stimulate essential physiological changes within the individuals involved.

For instance, humans come equipped with hormones (oxytocin and vasopressin) that promote trust and bonding. These hormone levels are raised when people engage in face-to-face conversations. Further, personal contact with others also stimulates two essential neurotransmitters in the brains of the parties involved. One is dopamine, which heightens attention and pleasure. The other is serotonin, which diminishes fear and worry.[19]

One can now begin to grasp why small group size is absolutely indispensable for the maintenance of intimate, trusting and supportive relationships vital for the free flow of new ideas and information. Without those close ties the hunter-gatherers would have had considerable difficulty in maintaining their successful lifestyles for as long as they did.

Our ancestors "innately" took competition by attraction rather than competition by intimidation to its absolute limits without ignoring the self-centered side of the people around them. They had no problem in fully tapping into the hidden wealth of their small social systems. Again, they practiced egalitarianism because it was the *most practical option* and not because they were noble unspoiled creatures of nature.

So, why and how should we apply the small very interdependent group framework of the hunter-gatherers to our 21st century organizations? I believe that has already become intuitively apparent but I will focus on five specific points. First, organizations desiring to be on the leading edge in any field that is dependent on knowledge work and workers need to make sure that their members do not work in groups or clans of more than 150 people. In addition, people within these "clans" must be encouraged to work in small free flowing teams similar to those of the foragers who did the actual hunting and gathering. I will discuss the concept of "real teams" in Chapter Four.

We must not forget that the wellspring of new innovative ideas is tacit knowledge, which can't be forced or managed out of people. It must be allowed to emerge through serendipitous interdependent relationships and interactions. These types of relationships can seldom take place between strangers since they are extraordinarily dependent on *continuously reinforced connections* between individuals who are committed to the same common goals.

Obviously, such tight associations can't be developed and maintained in large groups. We do have a tremendous capacity for complex social relationships. That capability, however, is by no means boundless. Thus, smart organizations will increase their effectiveness by not stretching the social connective capabilities of their members beyond the natural limits.

Second, close face-to-face encounters between people bring about positive physiological changes which promote trust and bonding and reduce fear and worry. What this means is that high, sustained levels of intellectual asset development can't be effectively accomplished in a totally virtual environment. This doesn't mean that technology, which allows us to establish virtual links globally, is useless. There is nothing wrong with virtual systems as long as the individuals involved thoroughly understand the reason why they must initially and then periodically engage in face-to-face exchanges. The invisible guiding hand of living systems is biological and not virtual.

Third, small close knit groups keep negative emotions and tensions, which narrow thought patterns by necessity, to a minimum. Thus, constructive relations generate positive emotions, which allow thinking to be more expansive and resourceful. In addition, heightened positive emotions and unrestricted thinking feed on each other making people even more creative over time and more emotionally balanced.[20] There is no question that self-organizing arrangements can become very powerful within a supportive environmental context. All one has to do is compare such systems to enterprises where the "boss" is constantly looking over people's shoulders and giving instructions.

Fourth, small group size is vital for the reduction of violence in our businesses and schools. Humans are innately supportive of one another as long as they have face-to-face relationships with each other and exist in a none-threatening trusting social environment where status and not rank is the key to success. Continued emphasis on various security measures and reliance on stricter rules in our schools and workplaces will not reduce violence appreciably. Although they are important elements in combating violence, they primarily deal with the symptoms rather than the real causes of the problem. Again, we need to stop trying to circumvent human nature.

Finally, for today's organizations to gain the full benefits from small group size, they must be very selective as to who is asked to join the clan. Remember that the hunter-gatherer groups were composed of relatives and *close friends*. Thus, in putting together a small and very collaborative work group one must assure that its members can form close ties. Without such ties people's altruistic tendencies will have difficulty in having an opportunity to be expressed. The member selection process is explained in more detail in Chapter Four.

Before I discuss the applicability of the next success factor of the foragers, I need to dispel one very common concern about small group size.

Many people I have spoken with about organizational dimensions generally agree that small size probably has a significant affect on creativity and productivity. However, they immediately voice their concerns about large firms like General Motors or Microsoft and how such institutions could possibly benefit from "smallness".

The good news is that a company can be both small and large simultaneously. For example, Asea Brown Boveri, an international electrical engineering company, has about 200,000 people on the payroll. Nonetheless, each of its roughly 5,000 independent operating units consists of an average of only fifty people and the organization as a whole is closely linked together as a network.

Another firm, W.L. Gore and Associates (best known for the invention of Gore-Tex which is widely used in outdoor clothing and camping gear), runs thirty-five manufacturing facilities with about 6,500 people around the world. None of their plants is operated with more than 200 associates. Gore has also never had a manager or boss in any of their operating units since the company was founded in 1958.

Maintained high, sustained levels of reciprocity, egalitarianism, and practiced consensus decision-making. Traveling on foot up to 2,500 miles a year within a large territory, and being fully dependent on the uncertainties presented by Mother Nature, took considerable courage and persistence. Yet, there is ample evidence that life for our hunter-gatherer ancestors was not as physically demanding as many people have assumed. In fact, most of their time was devoted to enjoying life in the company of friends and extended family members. That's not to say that life was easy without modern conveniences such as cars, grocery stores, pharmacies, hospitals, and waterproof camping gear. It obviously wasn't. However, there is now evidence that suggest that the lives of hunter-gatherers were less backbreaking than those of the early herders and farmers who followed them.

How was that possible when in today's "advanced" economies and especially in the United Sates a 24/7/365 work schedule is starting to become the standard? The answer to that question is quite straightforward—unadulterated teamwork. *The foragers lived in social groups where everyone knew where they had been, what needed to be taken care of at the moment, and where they were headed in the future.* There were no community secrets. Decisions were made by consensus assuring everyone's interests were taken into consideration as much as possible. Even their temporary campsites were designed to help maximize constant interaction.

There was no incentive to hoard or keep resources from other members of the band. Food couldn't be stored for long and personal items amounted to only what each individual could carry on their person. How could one hide his or her non-participation in a small group's activities when everything was out in the open? Furthermore, when everyone is a close friend or relative it makes little sense to resort to violence when disagreements arise. There was always an individual who could be trusted by both parties to help settle disputes that occurred. In essence, what made our ancestors so successful was that they thoroughly understood that the best option for survival was to work closely together instead of making the best of the circumstances independently.

The need for high, sustained levels of reciprocity and egalitarianism in today's organizations seem quite understandable. However, is it realistically attainable? It all depends on what an organization wants to accomplish in the long run. Under normal circumstances people will express their altruistic side only when they perceive themselves to be surrounded by a very supportive environment. Slogans and elaborate vision statements, which people know are there only to present a positive image, will not do the "trick". In fact, usually they have the opposite effect and only increase cynicism among organizational members.

So, a company or a school needs to decide whether they want to "control" the activities of their members by intimidation and all sorts of monetary incentives, or if they want to develop an organizational context that is very interdependent and supportive. A social institution must make a choice between the two options because they can't be mixed. In either case we can't circumvent human nature.

The first option will generate relatively high negative emotions and narrow thought patterns in addition to limiting the sharing of tacit knowledge. The second alternative will spawn more positive emotions stimulating more expansive and resourceful thinking, increase the levels of social capital, not to mention a much greater sharing of tacit knowledge. We must also remember that knowledge is an infinite not a finite resource. The more it is shared the more it grows. Thus, reciprocity is as vital today as it was in the ancient past.

Members owned their own means of production. This is a critical success factor of the hunter-gatherers. It seems like an oxymoron but true mutuality and interdependence requires that the parties involved are also considerably independent. If an individual isn't capable of producing or contributing something on their own then they are to a large degree dependent on the will and resources of others. Hence, such a person really can't be a full-fledged member of a team since their contributions will be insignificant.

Let me use an example to demonstrate my point. In a real partnership each party brings something valuable to the table, otherwise it wouldn't be a partnership. However, the item of value can be just about anything that makes a partnership viable. It can be equipment, money, specific knowledge or skills and so on.

Hence, a real team is composed of full-fledged partners, each capable of making significant contributions to the success of the team. Essentially, reciprocity is about interdependence, not dependence. By owning their own weapons, tools and other personal gear, foragers could decide whether to function independently or as part of a larger party. Therefore, when they joined a group they became a partner, not a hired hand.

That is precisely why organizations today need to begin to treat their knowledge professionals as partners and not as employees or hired hands. They can be junior or senior partners, but they must feel that have a say in how the entire enterprise is run and not just be responsible for their individual tasks. Like our ancestors, they also own their own means of production—their talents, knowledge, and skills. It is not only a "nicer" but a lot more effective way to run an organization in today's environment.

Emphasized individual autonomy and self-reliance tempered with social responsibility and accountability. A high degree of individual autonomy existed among the hunter-gatherers. This aspect, of course, goes hand-in-hand with the fact that they owned their own means of production. Every person was expected to be self-reliant to one degree or another. At the same time, however, everyone had an intrinsic desire to be responsible and accountable for the overall success of the clan because their own success depended on it.

Again, without a considerable degree of individual autonomy, genuine teamwork and interdependence would have been impossible. In a true partnership there are no entitlements. Each person assumed full responsibility not only for their efforts but also for the accomplishments or failures of the entire band.

Is this not exactly what we "desire" from all members of an organization currently but seldom attain? We rarely achieve it today because the people in charge are usually afraid to provide the necessary individual autonomy to organizational members, thinking the subordinates may not know how to use it properly.

In reality the opposite is true when you have the proper organizational context and assemble self-reliant responsible people (associates, not hired hands). By giving up "perceived" control (perceived because people really can't be controlled as explained in the next chapter) you actually gain more control or, rather, positive order. Our ancestors understood that fact. Are we less intelligent?

Practiced situational or shared leadership and there were no status differences between the sexes. The hunter-gatherers relied on situational leadership based on expertise (social attention holding power) rather than rank (resource holding power) and on equality among men and women because those, again, were the best options. In self-organizing societies, where reciprocity reigned, position power and discrimination made little sense.

Leadership was fluid and situational. People sought advice and paid attention to individuals who had developed a reputation for certain talents or skills when a specific problem or opportunity arose. Although labor was fairly divided, since men did most of the hunting and women principally gathered, the division was practical and not inflexible. Consequently, women were as independent as the men and also assumed leadership roles depending on the situation and their particular expertise.

Once more it is relatively obvious how we can apply these two success factors of the foragers in our current social institutions. If we agree that self-organization or unmanagement (openly nurturing the power of informal groups and networks within an enterprise) is the best option for running knowledge intensive organizations, then position power and discrimination of any kind are roadblocks to success and should be eliminated. The subject of leadership is covered in-depth in Chapter Six.

Generating high sustained levels of intellectual capital is all about voluntary interdependent connections between people instead of a few chosen people wielding power over others. We need to remind ourselves that knowledge is an infinite resource and, therefore, should be shared as much as possible to make it expand more rapidly.

Before I explain the fundamental reasons why most of today's social institutions are operated in a top down hierarchical manner, I need to first clarify the physiological reasons why our hunter-gatherer ancestors were able to operate successfully in the open self-organizing mode for so long. A quick look at our innate drives or genetic predispositions will help to accomplish that.

5.   OUR GENETIC PREDISPOSITIONS

We must keep in mind that our behavior evolved first and that the ability to make sense of it developed later. If that were not the case modern humans most probably wouldn't exist today. Life forms have evolved to cope with specific immediate environmental conditions and not for general purposes. The evolutionary process is incapable of anticipating the future and, therefore, never "wastes" vital resources to give an organism some capacity that it can't use immediately.

Therefore, we need to realize that the genetic predispositions or innate drives of modern humans evolved eons ago to help us cope with life in small hunter-gatherer societies on the African Savannah way before our kind eventually migrated to all the other continents. Our genetic tendencies are the very foundation of how we interact with one another. Namely, they are the core of the continuous self-organizing process that takes place as we get together with other individuals and groups.

Innate drives are not pure instincts. They are much broader. For example, we blink when something unexpectedly flashes by our eyes or we jump when a loud noise startles us. These are instinctive reactions. With innate drives we have much more leeway in how we respond. For instance, we all crave for fatty, sweet and salty foods but we do have free will (some of us more than others) to override those yearnings. These are innate drives because they "nudge" (as opposed to direct) us to behave in a certain way in response to specific environmental conditions. Food processors are well aware of these tendencies. All you need to do is check the salt and fat contents on the next bag of potato chips you buy.

Researchers have concluded that about fifty percent of an individual's potential for behavior is inherited, including the potential for happiness and morality. That is precisely why a person's personality doesn't fluctuate much over a life span. Hence, we are all born with certain "base line" inherited predispositions or set points. These set points are also referred to as ultimate causes.

The good news is that there is quite a range on either side of these genetic set points. Thus, the other fifty percent of the equation is played out through life experiences. These environmental affects are called proximate causes. What this means, for example, is that if you were born as a relatively gloomy individual you will never be a real party animal. However, that doesn't mean you can't work on getting into the high end of your happiness range.

So, what are some of our foremost inherited predispositions or innate drives? Innate drives come in two major categories. Multiple authors have given these categories different names.[21] I have simply labeled them *self-centered* and *other-centered*. Recall that several hundred million years ago our ancestors fended for themselves independently and later lived in small groups where rank was an important factor for success. The instincts and innate drives that evolved in those distant environments are still part of our make-up. They generally represent the self-centered side of our predispositions.

Within the past ten million years evolution began to give those organisms who maximized their friendships and minimized their antagonisms an advantage. This, of course, includes our kind. The innate drives of this period mostly embody the other-centered side of our predispositions. Now let's take a more detailed look at these two general categories of innate drives and how they are affected by different environmental conditions.

Looking at Figure 3-1, and for the moment ignoring the arrows, we can observe that some of the self-centered drives on the left side are more instinctive than others. For instance, the concerns for domination, territory and mating or sex evolved 300 million years ago and are, therefore, more instinctive behaviors. The predispositions to read other people's minds and to deceive others and ourselves came much later and are less instinctive.[22]

Most of the other-centered innate drives on the right side of Figure 3-1 are self-explanatory. The exceptions may be the last three. As an example, we usually experience a deep sense of remorse when something tragic happens to a family member or friend. Further, we feel shame when we can't meet the expectations of other people. Also, when we break certain agreed upon rules or standards we experience guilt. All three predispositions appear to have evolved to help maintain group cohesion without the need to resort to intimidation.

It's also important to remember that, in general, there isn't one particular gene for every predisposition. For instance, no specific gene exists for concern with attachment or domination. Our bodies are *parallel operating systems* where every component works together simultaneously. Thus, all of our genes, cells and neurons work in concert with one another. Some genes may have a more dominant role than others in certain behaviors but usually none plays an all-inclusive part.

As mentioned in Chapter Two, it is vital that we keep in mind that we are *not* dealing with genetic determinism. Rather, as Colin Tudge makes clear,

> "...we should be prepared to use our brains to override 'nature.' We should seek to ensure that our brains...are the ultimate arbiters. But we should not underestimate nature. Our inherited nature *includes* much of what any of us would call morality; it *includes* a respect for fellow creatures. So although we might override nature, we would do well to listen to nature too. We all know what 'conscience' is: the 'inner voice' that tells us we are behaving badly. We need not doubt that that 'inner voice' is itself evolved, calling to us from our difficult days on the African plains."[23]

Understanding that fifty percent of our behavior is genetically based helps us in five general ways. First, knowing that we are born with two archetypical behavioral modes allows us to better anticipate the needs and behavior of people under various environmental conditions.

For instance, people immersed in a very competitive, position power and compliance oriented organization will behave and think in a certain way no matter what they say in public or what is formally requested. Asking people to be good team players in such a context is foolish. Such an achievement is "genetically" impossible unless the company's facilities catch on fire and even then it may be doubtful.

Second, no two individuals can respond exactly the same way to a particular problem or opportunity no matter how closely their genetic behavioral set points match.[24] As an example, two people who find themselves in the surroundings described above will express their anger differently. The one with a relatively high predisposition for anger will most likely express his or her frustrations more often and more vehemently. The other, who is also experiencing lots of dissatisfaction, will convey his or her feelings in a more restrained way even when they are at the very high end of their anger set point.

Third, fully grasping the duality of our innate drives permits us to design organizational constructs that support voluntary cooperative behavior instead of hindering it. Even when we choose to operate some of our social institutions in a very compliance oriented top down style we need to be aware of the impact such an environment has on our inherited predispositions. Why, for instance, does the average employee only work at two-thirds of his or her capacity? Why is worker loyalty so low?

Fourth, it is essential to realize that our innate drives can't be circumvented. They are there no matter what kind of a setting we find ourselves in. Yes, there is a range on either side of the genetic set points but beyond that range the drives can't be manipulated. We can change the organizational setting but we can't change our innate drives.

That is why, for example, the movie producers, advertising agencies and the media in general focus on sex and violence. These subject matters impact our most basic predispositions (on our self-centered side) that evolved hundreds of millions of years ago and which are most easily activated. Our other-centered drives, which developed much later, take more effort to be fully expressed.

Finally, humans function best in an environment where both the self-centered and the other centered drives have a chance to be expressed. Fostering both sides of human nature is a vital success factor for our kind. We do not have a "good" and a "bad" side. Both sets are an integral part of our being and work together to give us the best opportunity to meet the common goal of all living systems.[25]

Thus, every social institution should strive to develop and maintain an organizational context where both sides of human innate drives have an opportunity to be expressed in a *balanced* fashion. Our hunter-gatherer ancestors used that balance to their advantage and that is precisely why they were so successful for so long. I will explain this in more detail in Chapter Four.

In the final analysis during the course of evolution the human mind didn't give up instincts but instead expanded them in becoming more adept in dealing with social complexity.[26] Hence, appropriate behavior is the province of our innate drives set by evolutionary selection and our life experiences. They are the internal criteria that guide us to take certain kinds of action or to ignore others as we continuously scan and categorize the activities around us.

6.   EXPRESSING OUR INNATE DRIVES

Figure 3-1 is also a simplified portrayal of how our innate drives are expressed or not expressed. As stated above, about fifty percent of an individual's potential for behavior is inherited. What this means is that we are all born with certain baseline genetic tendencies or behavioral set points.

Of course, the other half of our inclinations is molded by life experiences, providing us a relatively wide range of mannerisms around the inherited set points. Therefore, if an individual is born with a rather high predisposition for anger they can work on subduing it in various situations but they will still have a fairly elevated "trigger-point" compared to most other people.

Let us take a closer look at Figure 3-1 to determine what it indicates about our behavioral expression process. At the outset, we need to comprehend what the dissimilar arrows depict. First, the length of an arrow indicates the strength of a particular drive. As such, it is quite evident that no two drives have equal "force" behind them and unsurprisingly no two people inherit the exact sets of drives.

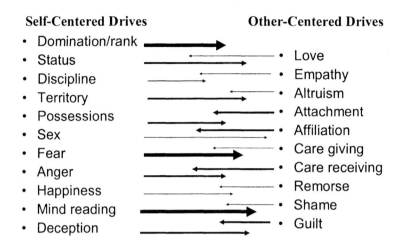

Self-Centered Drives

- Domination/rank
- Status
- Discipline
- Territory
- Possessions
- Sex
- Fear
- Anger
- Happiness
- Mind reading
- Deception

Other-Centered Drives

- Love
- Empathy
- Altruism
- Attachment
- Affiliation
- Care giving
- Care receiving
- Remorse
- Shame
- Guilt

Figure 3-1. Expression of Innate Human Drives

Second, the thickness of an arrow illustrates the frequency of a drive's expression or use by a person. For example, the diagram shows that this fictitious individual lives or works in an environment that impacts his or her concerns for domination, fear, and mind reading quite persistently while many of the other drives have essentially atrophied from lack of activity.

This is a very important consideration when we deal with change in general. As one can see from the thickness of the arrows in the diagram, change is not only a mental but also a physiological process. Therefore, considerable time, effort, and practice are required before a person, team or an entire organization becomes comfortable with new procedures and operations. Thus, the old saying, "Use it or lose it," is applicable to everything we do or don't do.

Third, the head of an arrow in Figure 3-1 indicates the set points for a given innate drive. Accordingly, life experiences (50 percent of a person's behavioral potential) can reduce or extend the influence of a drive by half its depicted length but cannot change the set point itself. That is precisely why an individual's personality fluctuates little over a life span.[27]

Finally, it is also important to visualize that both sets of innate human drives need to be expressed in a balanced manner, as shown by the opposing and overlapping arrows, in order for a person to function normally. We must also keep in mind that our genetic drives can't be consciously controlled. They only respond to various environmental conditions.

"So to the degree that all traits are hereditary, they are adaptive; they are helpful to survival. Every trait then, whether it is anger or reliability, solitude or defiance, has its survival value."[28] Therefore, we need to live and labor in social contexts where there is ample opportunity for our self-centered, as well as the other-centered, drives to be mutually expressed.

Further, we need to keep in mind that including the influence of our genes in the "behavioral equation" has nothing to do with *determinism*. That is, we can't blame our actions on human nature or suggest that, "The genes made me do it." Steven Pinker explains it best:

> For one thing, genes cannot pull the strings of behavior directly. Behavior is caused by the activity of the brain, and the most genes can do is affect its wiring, size, shape and sensitivity to hormones and other molecules. Among the brain circuits laid down by genes are the ones that reflect on memories, current circumstances and the anticipated consequences of various courses of action and that select behavior accordingly—in an intricate and not entirely predictable way. These circuits are what we call "free will," and providing them with information about the likely consequences of behavioral options is what we call "holding people responsible."[29]

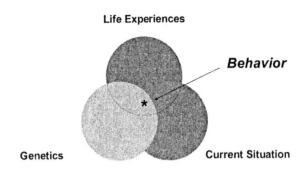

Life Experiences

Behavior

Genetics   Current Situation

Figure 3-2. Dynamics of Human Behavior

As a synopsis, Figure 3-2 graphically illustrates the general dynamics of human behavior. Fundamentally, our actions and reactions consist of the fluid interfaces of three factors—our life experiences, our genetic predispositions and the immediate situation(s) we are facing. Thus, how we behave depends on our *perceptions* of the people and circumstances we come upon, modified by our innate drives which, in turn, are molded by the events we encounter throughout our lives.

I suggest that the reader take a few moments to reflect on the day-to-day events that take place in their current workplace and also recollect activities in some of the past organizations they were associated with in order to "very generally" determine how those episodes impacted their innate drives. For instance, is/was one of the sides expressed more than the other? Why was that? How much did the organizational context in the different companies or divisions allow both sides of the drives to be expressed in a balanced manner? Which predispositions were activated most often and which essentially atrophied? How did all that enhance or deter your commitment and productivity? You may also want to speculate as to how these same conditions affected the drives of several of your friends and colleagues.

7.   THE CURRENT PREDICAMENT

Both nature and our own kind have contributed to the collapse of the most successful and longitudinal human social adaptation to date, the hunter-gatherer way of life. How could such a thriving system give way to something new? Well, it happened very slowly and the general structure that began to gradually dominate most forms of social relationships was not really new. In fact, it was many millions of years older than the arrangement that it pushed aside.

The disintegration of the self-organizing or unmanagement systems of the foragers got its start at the end of the last Ice Age roughly eighteen thousand years ago. The enormous northern ice sheets receded rapidly (relatively speaking) in approximately six thousand years or so, causing oceans to rise dramatically to roughly present day levels.[30]

As a consequence, the plant and animal life around the world changed significantly except on the African Savannah. Hence, our ancient relatives were forced to make major adjustments in their diets as scores of the large mammals favored by the hunters for millennia steadily disappeared. As a result, they began to consume a greater mixture of smaller animals, more plant food and seafood.

What had an even more drastic social impact was that with the flooding of the coastal lowlands and rapidly spreading forests the hunter-gatherers were constrained to smaller and smaller geographic areas and, therefore, became less mobile. As travel became more restricted and demanding, populations also grew in these enclaves. This, in turn, led to the founding of agriculture and the domestication of animals. Thus, the stage was set for the proliferation of increasingly larger and more complex societies, but at a considerable cost which we are still paying today.

Paradoxically, evolution has not endowed us with brains capable of innately keeping track of more than 150 people. Consequently, beyond that range larger "civilizations" were incapable of maintaining *voluntary* cooperation and needed another organizational form to facilitate the coordination of activities of increasingly larger numbers of people. As a result, the social system that first appeared roughly 200 million years ago again became the rage. Rank and the hierarchy began to creep back in.

The changeover was so gradual that hardly anyone became aware of the shift. It was similar to global warming of today that many people still doubt is actually taking place. One might guess that the biggest culprits were the excess accumulation of resources and greed. Is there a better way to survive long enough to pass on ones genes to the next generation than to have many more resources than one reasonably needs? Is that part of human nature? Yes, it all depends on the social and organizational contexts that we develop and live in.

Uninhibited self-indulgence is still widespread even today as exemplified by organizations such as Enron, WorldCom, Adelphia Communications, AOL Time Warner, Dynergy, Global Crossing and a host of others. Again, we must keep in mind that *capitalism without a strong sense of community ultimately leads to unrestrained greed.* A more thorough and realistic grasp of human nature would allow us to minimize many of these problems.

8. FUNDAMENTAL RESOURCE ACQUISITION AND DISTRIBUTION MODES

A more comprehensive look at our three fundamental resource and acquisition modes, mentioned throughout this chapter, will help to tie up possible loose ends and also aid in better understanding some of the concepts presented later in the book. Essentially, one or a combination of these modes is activated when people interact with one another in quest of scarce resources. Which mode dominates depends on the situation that individuals perceive themselves to be in. Clearly, the three survival modes are intimately linked to our innate drives. Hence, how people's innate drives are expressed or not expressed under varying circumstances has a direct influence on their resource acquisition mode selection process.

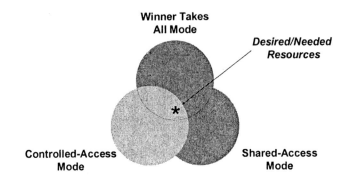

Figure 3-3. Resource Acquisition and Distribution Modes

Figure 3-3 portrays the dynamic relationships and activation of our three fundamental resource acquisition and distribution modes. The process begins with a *perceived* (real or imagined) threat or opportunity as an individual or group scans the environment for desired resources and how best to obtain them. As depicted by the model, the focus of the overlapping resource acquisition methods is on the desired or needed resources. Clearly, the relationships between the modes are dynamic indicating that more than one mode can be expressed at a time if necessary. I'll come back to this point in a moment but first let me define the three modes depicted in the illustration.

The *winner-takes-all mode* is set in motion at the individual level. Some groups also appear to use this mode but they have an additional requirement which is to distribute the "spoils" to its members once they have been acquired. Because groups need to have a means of allocating their attained resources to its affiliates, that puts them in one of the other two categories of survival modes that I will describe momentarily.

So, in the winner-takes-all mind-set individuals involved pull out all the stops, including the use of force or violence if necessary, in satisfying their needs or desires. Also, by definition the victor doesn't share the winnings with anyone other than possibly his/her immediate family. In effect, after more than 300 million years of evolution this aggressive mode of self-preservation is still imprinted on our genes and can surface given the right conditions. We should never forget that we're not fundamentally "noble savages" by any stretch of the imagination. Thus, we can be both the most brutal and altruistic beings in the world depending on the environmental conditions we find ourselves in.

The hierarchy began to appear about 200 million years ago when certain species found it more beneficial to live in groups controlled by a pecking order. Within this framework one or a handful of individuals manage and control the access to all the resources of a social institution. Hence, I have named this type of resource management structure the *controlled-access system*. Ironically, only recently (in the past 15,000 years or so) has the controlled-access mode of resource acquisition and distribution slowly regained its dominance among our kind, reaching its zenith during the Industrial Age.

Recall that reciprocity and interdependence were major success factors for the hunter-gatherer. Hence, *everyone* was responsible for managing the clan's resources equitably. In other words, access to needed resources wasn't controlled by any particular person or persons but was shared. That's why I've labeled this mode of resource management the *shared-access system*. Essentially, these entities are overt self-organizing systems that function through shared leadership and consensus decision-making.

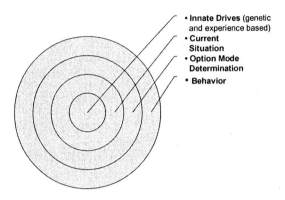

Figure 3-4. Dynamics of Survival Option Selection and Expression

As depicted by Figure 3-4, the selection and expression of a survival or resource acquisition mode option(s) is a very dynamic and fluid process. That is, all of the four key factors included in the diagram come into play almost simultaneously. As one can observe, the primary initiator of the course(s) of action are our innate drives as modified by individual personal experiences (fundamentally a person's personality) and how the drives are affected by one's immediate environmental context. Thus, in what manner a person or group will react to a given situation can't be easily predicted nor channeled.

At this juncture a couple of hypothetical examples of how the three modes are expressed in an organizational setting should help further clarify their differences and dynamic interrelationships. Let's start with a controlled-access mode. In an attempt to "control" an unexpected situation an administrator tells a subordinate to immediately transfer certain scarce materials to another department. The individual refuses to carry out the directive insisting that such an action makes little sense. The administrator threatens the individual with instant dismissal. The subordinate takes a swing at the administrator and a fight ensues. The controlled-access mode has suddenly turned into a winner-takes-all mode.

This simple example demonstrates a key characteristic of a controlled-access system. When a superior issues an order to a subordinate(s) that person has only two ways to respond. They can either fight or take flight. That is, they either stand their ground hoping their views will be heard (which may or may not turn into a winner-takes-all confrontation) or submit to the will of the supervisor, which is a form of flight. Right or wrong, tall or flat a hierarchy isn't an ideal organizational framework for consensus decision-making.

Now let's take a similar example using the shared-access context. A shared-access system is dependent on joint leadership but not on bosses and bossing. That is to say, leadership is based on talent, experience, and a proven track record rather than position power (Chapter Six is entirely devoted to leadership). Hence, when a problem (or opportunity) appears it's the responsibility of the first person(s) who becomes aware of it to take the lead or to assure that the most knowledgeable people in the subject area become involved. There is no argument as to who is in charge because everyone is responsible and accountable for the success of the organization. Key decisions are made by consensus rather than by decrees from the top, since each person has a stake in the outcome.

❑ **Winner Takes All Mode (Power Base: Individual Means—300million years ago to present)**
  Advantage-Personal choice
  Disadvantage-Competition and aggression
  Cost Effectiveness-Low
  Optimum Group Size-1 or 2 people (immediate family)
❑ **Controlled-Access Mode (Power Base: Group Rank or Resource Holding Power—200 million years ago to present)**
  Advantage-Hierarchical control (compliance)
  Disadvantage-High psychological tension
  Cost Effectiveness-moderate
  Optimum Group Size-More than 150 people
❑ **Shared-Access Mode (Power Base: Recognized Expertise or Social Attention Holding Potential—10 million years ago to present)**
  Advantage-Voluntary cooperation (commitment)
  Disadvantage-Maintenance of common vision/goals
  Cost Effectiveness-High
  Optimum Group Size-Less than 150 people

Figure 3-5. Resource Acquisition and Distribution Modes Summary

As summarized in Figure 3-5, each of the three resource acquisition and distribution modes has its particular advantage, disadvantage, cost effectiveness, and optimal group size where it can be best applied. In the winner-takes-all mode the advantage is that access to resources is not controlled by designated others (a hierarchy) and that the resources don't need to be shared with anyone else other then possibly immediate kin. Also, individuals are free to make their own decisions/choices without concern for others.

The disadvantage of this mode is that it usually leads to fierce competition and possible violence. Further, working individually typically leads to low cost effectiveness in acquiring required resources and limits optimum group size to no more than the size of a family. Humans are mainly social animals and, therefore, going it alone has huge drawbacks. Nevertheless, after more than 300 million years of evolution the winner-takes-all mode is still imprinted on our genes and does surface given the right conditions.

The advantage of the controlled-access mode of social interaction is that collective activities can be controlled and coordinated, to a degree, by one or a handful of individuals. Essentially, order is maintained chiefly through compliance or resource holding power, rather than commitment, as lower ranking group members follow instructions emanating from the top. In addition, group size can be expanded beyond 150 people.

The disadvantage of this mode is that there is always some level of psychological tension created by the "policing" actions (intimidation) of individuals with higher position power. Also, the level of cost effectiveness in acquiring resources is relatively moderate but higher than compared to the winner-takes-all mode. The reasons for the moderate cost effectiveness stem from the fact that not everyone works at maximum capacity in such groups since reciprocity is not prevalent and considerable energy is spent in both circumventing the hierarchy and competing for higher rank.

The shared-access system seems to be the best resource acquisition and distribution mode for groups of about 150 members or less. It's also the most cost effective approach because all activities are accomplished through voluntary collaboration or commitment and status based on social attention holding potential rather than obedience to rank. Thus, energy that is normally expended by people vying for more powerful positions and circumventing the chain of command is directed towards more socially productive goals.

Of course, a drawback to this mode of operation is that it takes considerable effort to assure that everyone involved remains committed to the agreed upon common vision and goals. Also, if large organizations are to benefit from the effectiveness of shared-access systems they need to be segmented into relatively autonomous groups of not more than 150 members.

Based on what I have presented so far, I believe we only have two very general means available to us for organizing our collective endeavors— *shared-access and controlled-access systems*—if we discount the individual winner-takes-all mode as quite impractical for long term success. Yes, there are almost limitless variations that can be developed under each category but, from my perspective, there are no other broad options accessible to us.

What is most interesting is that given a choice most people prefer to live and work in a shared-access environment. Why? The reason for that is quite simple. A shared-access social context provides the best opportunity for people to be able to express their innate drives in a balanced fashion. This will become increasingly apparent as we progress through the chapters that follow.

9.   SUCCESS IN THE FUTURE

Undoubtedly, knowledge professionals will be the predominant force in the future, especially in the industrialized countries. What other advantage than the generation of intellectual capital do developed nations have? It certainly isn't in manufacturing. Any nation in the world can now acquire the latest manufacturing technology (including training) literally overnight if they have the capital and desire to do so. In addition, low wages not only of blue-collar employees but also of highly educated and skilled personnel in less developed countries are forcing businesses to take their work off-shore at an ever accelerating pace.

Only rising levels of overall innovation and entrepreneurship will help companies in industrialized nations to maintain a competitive edge in the global marketplace. Thus, increasing the innovative capacity and productivity of knowledge workers, by explicitly supporting the activities of the informal networks within organizations and the wise use of information technology, will be the key to success in the future. In order to accomplish that, however, we need to first have a good grasp of the underpinnings and dynamics of human nature. As professor Richard Florida has concluded:

The economic leaders of the future will not necessarily be emerging giants like India and China. They certainly won't be countries that focus on being cost-effective centers for manufacturing and basic business processing. Rather, they will be the countries that are able to attract creative people and come up with next-generation products and business processes as a result.[31]

In the next chapter I will discuss the difference between control versus order and the organizational options that differentiation leads to. Consequently, we will be better able to determine what organizational frameworks will be best suited for the Knowledge Age that we have entered.

Chapter 4

FOSTERING POSITIVE ORDER

Knowing the distinction between control and order can make the difference as to whether or not an organization succeeds or fails in the new millennium. That is especially true for enterprises that are heavily dependent on the continuous generation of intellectual assets. Such companies must be capable of attracting and keeping top notch knowledge professionals motivated if they want to prolong their existence. Without a thorough grasp of the distinction between control, and order in addition to the vital importance of self-organization in our lives, that is almost an impossible undertaking.

Regrettably, what the majority of people around the world still fail to grasp is that all living systems, including our kind, have evolved to function in a self-organizing mode 24 hours a day, seven days a week, and 365 days a year. Harder yet to fathom is the fact that even people in prisons, gulags, concentration camps and very tightly run top down organizations continuously self-organize in response to the demands of their immediate surroundings and conditions.

Well-seasoned individuals have intuitively understood this fact ever since modern humans first appeared on our planet. The "formal" discovery, however, that people self-organize continuously had to wait until the Hawthorne Studies were conducted at the Western Electric Company in the late 1920s and early 1930s. The "newly" discovered phenomenon was labeled the *informal organization* and was said to be unavoidable and uncontrollable in any social entity. The studies also concluded that an informal organization may or may not support the formal goals pursued by a particular institution.[1]

This poses a very fundamental but critical question. "If informal organizations are a fact of life, then why is it not one of the major topics for scrutiny in our executive suites?" Ignoring this reality certainly seems to make little sense. If self-organization is inevitable and irrepressible, then doesn't it make more sense to take advantage of the occurrence and its associated factors rather than doing the impossible by attempting to circumvent it or driving it underground?

Accordingly, in this chapter I begin to examine self-organization more closely leading to a more in-depth analysis of the phenomenon in the next chapter. My overall goal is to illustrate how we can foster and leverage this extraordinary and naturally occurring process within our organizations.

1.   FUNDAMENTALS OF SELF-ORGANIZATION

To begin with, all living systems constantly self-organize in response to the conditions of their immediate surroundings. Conversely, from a practical societal perspective, inanimate objects and structures don't, although in theory they do at the atomic and sub-atomic levels. Our focus, however, is on people and social institutions and not on quantum physics.

Self-organization begins at the molecular level of an individual and extends to his or her contact with the environment. For example, the 30 to 40 thousand genes in the human genome don't provide a specific wiring diagram for the development of a person. Rather, the genetic code imposes a set of restraints on the growth process.

Genes work together in a self-organizing mode in order to create a human being. Thus, no two people, even identical twins, are ever completely alike. If, for instance, each gene were responsible for the development of a single element of a body, the genome would run out of genes before it had helped to assemble an arm.[2]

The same is true of the trillions of body cells and the billions of neurons of our brains. They all work together simultaneously with the assistance of the genes in accomplishing a common purpose without a "boss". That is, the entire system organizes itself, except there is no agent within the system doing the organizing, assuring that the mind and body function properly and survive long enough to perpetuate the species. In turn, a person, when they come in contact with other individuals and groups, reacts and interacts with them as well as they can to accomplish the same common purpose.

Without getting too technical, we must bear in mind that *everything* we do mentally, physically and in maintaining our bodily functions is accomplished through the expression or suppression of our genes. Paradoxically, genetic changes take millions of years to incorporate into our genetic structures; however, environmental impact on gene expression is instantaneous. Therefore, the focus of our social institutions should be on developing and maintaining systems that support the self-organizing processes *naturally* occurring in any organization instead of continuously trying to control the behavior of people.

Self-organization at all levels takes place through the process of *circular causality*. As portrayed by the circles in Figure 4-1, what this means is that as one cell, person or group affects another cell, person or group they, in turn, are also affected by those encountered entities. These interactions are mutually reinforcing and intensify over time, held together by a common survival strategy. Circular causality, of course, is a never-ending process and continues until there is a disconnection between the parties involved.

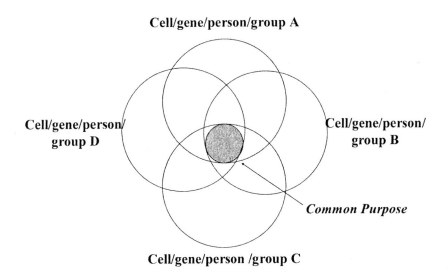

Figure 4-1. Circular Causality

More specifically, at the social level dyads and peer networks consist of self-reliant autonomous members. Each person reacts individually according to internal rules (instincts, innate drives, experience, culture, needs, etc.) and the conditions of their immediate surroundings. The interacting people are well connected but not through some centralized hub or authority.[3] All you have to do is reminisce the last time you became acquainted with a stranger and the dynamic processes that ensued as the two of you learned to know each other more closely.

Thus, order is achieved through an "invisible guiding hand" that keeps the system together by achieving coordination without control. Ironically, this applies to any organizational construct but that does not mean that the end results are the same. Namely, self-organization takes place as readily in a shared-access system as it does in a controlled-access environment. The difference is that in the former the informal networks evolve relatively openly and mainly support overall institutional goals, whereas in the latter they operate quite clandestinely and their activities may oppose officially advocated objectives. Now we can begin to grasp why it makes sense to control machines and other such inanimate frameworks but not people or social groups.

2.   CONTROL VERSUS ORDER

As you recall, concern for discipline is one of our innate drives on the self-centered side. That is, all of us to one degree or another want to have reasonable power over the day-to-day activities of our lives. Very simply, everyone has an overall genetic predisposition to make every effort to live their lives in as secure, predictable, and comfortable surroundings as possible. Hence, our desire to maintain "law and order" around us is part of our general inclination. Interestingly, as suggested in the previous chapter, there are only two sensible ways to achieve that state of being, which I will explain momentarily. In either case, self-organization is part of the equation, although the means to the end and their effectiveness differ considerably.

At the individual and dyad levels. In looking at discipline or personal power it will also become apparent that all the other self-centered drives are intricately involved. This again demonstrates how everything in the human system works together concurrently. A moment of reflection on our past experiences allows us to relate to the fact that a person, in reality, only has two primary options in attaining and maintaining a "sense" of control around them when dealing with another person—*intimidation (domination/rank) or consensus (altruism/reciprocity).*

If the first alternative is selected then an individual needs to perceive that they wield some form of power over the person or persons involved. That power, of course, comes in various categories such as physical strength, possessions, knowledge, connections, job retention, and the like.

When using domination or intimidation in trying to control others, what are the results? Flight or fight. A person either submits to the demands of another individual (which is a form of flight), withdraws from the engagement altogether or they, in turn, resort to intimidation in kind (fight). Let's say an individual submits to the demands or threats. Does that mean the initiator of the confrontation has attained control of the situation? Hardly. The originator of the altercation will only have shifted the balance of power for the moment. In reality, the problem has not been resolved since the "vanquished" will surely strive to retain their own sense of personal power and status by some other means or find a way around the aggressor.

We must bear in mind that all of us have an inborn need to protect our individual psychological and physical turf (even violently) when we perceive we are threatened. It is a deep-seated trait that our distant ancestors acquired about 400 million years ago and that we have inherited. Anger, like fear, is a potent force once expressed and difficult to quench.

In addition, self-esteem plays a major role in social relationships. Therefore, if the situation prevails for some time the submissive person may also begin to suffer from low self-esteem and stress, which can then lead to depression (a form of escape). That certainly isn't a very productive and healthy state of affairs in any organization. It's no wonder violent outbursts are becoming more frequent in our workplaces and schools.

We should also be cognizant of the fact that there are four primary sources for malice or motives for individuals to act in ways which others will identify as "evil."[4] One is the longing for material goods that includes money and power. These ends are not really erroneous by themselves but rather the means in how they are attained can have dire consequences. Threatened egotism is the second basis of unacceptable behavior that causes harm to others. "The people (or groups or countries) most prone to violence are the ones who are most susceptible to ego threats, especially those who have inflated, exalted opinions of themselves or whose normally high self-esteem does occasionally take a nosedive."

The third source of evil is obsessive idealism. Hence, such individuals or groups feel justified in using what ever means necessary "against the seemingly evil forces that oppose them." The pursuit of sadistic pleasure is the final source of malice. Fortunately, only five to six percent of perpetrators get their kicks out of such acts as rape and torture. Why are cruelty and tyranny not more common? "The answer is that violent impulses are typically restrained by inner inhibitions; people exercise self-control to avoid lashing out at others every time they might feel like it."

So, can you truly *control* people? Not really. You can only restrict the *visible behavior* (not the activities of the mind) of individuals for a time or worse, precipitate violence or mental instability through relentless domination. After all, humans have evolved to be completely capable of functioning independently when they wish to do so instead of having to be constantly "bossed around" by somebody. We tend to forget (at times knowingly but I believe mostly unconsciously) that people have evolved to be self-reliant organisms and, therefore, should be treated accordingly. What about the use of consensus to gain a "sense" of control in our lives? Consensus brings mutuality into play. Thus, the expression of our genetic predispositions shifts partially away from the self-centered side and begins to also include the other-centered side. That is, the duality of human nature now has the opportunity to be expressed in a balanced manner.

In effect, the parties involved need to have come to the realization that solving problems and taking advantage of opportunities in the long run demands that they work together, not against one another. This means that whatever decisions are made must be mutually beneficial requiring high levels of interdependence and reciprocity.

Essentially, instead of pursuing unfeasible control, the parties concerned seek to attain *dynamic order* in their reciprocally advantageous relationship. The key word here is "dynamic". Order delineates fluidity and motion (circular causality), which is the foundation of self-organization. Control, on the other hand, is a static concept applicable to machines and other inanimate objects, but not to living systems. Hence, control by no means equates to order. Realistically, we can only talk about self-control and not externally imposed control.

Moreover, *positive dynamic order*, as opposed to *negative dynamic order* created by domination or other threatening conditions, has an impact on two vital innate drives needed to be expressed in mutually beneficial relationships—status and attachment. As stated before, the maintenance of self-esteem of all the parties concerned in a collaborative relationship is extremely important. Positive dynamic order supports that. Everyone involved feels that they are a key contributor or a true partner in the affair.

As a result, individuals participating in an event all uphold their status (a self-centered drive) based on expertise and not rank or position power. Also, without the concern for rank, people are free to work on mutually rewarding relationships and in the process satisfy their need for attachment (an other-centered drive). In essence, the more opportunities people have to exercise self-control the more *committed and proactive* they will become. Conversely, the more external controls are placed on individuals, the more *compliance oriented and passive* they will turn out to be. You may want to re-examine Figure 3-2 in order to get graphic illustration summarizing what I've discussed above.

In a controlled-access organizational context. Now let us examine how self-organization takes place when rank and imposed controls are used at the organizational level. That is, when one or a select few individuals control the access to all the key institutional resources while everyone else must provide in-depth justification whenever they need to gain access to these assets.

Unfortunately, this manner of running social groups has intensified in the past 15,000 years to the point where most people today believe that there is no other alternative. However, as I pointed out in the previous chapter, there is another option that our kind has used very successfully for 99 percent of their existence. Nevertheless, instructions imprinted in our genetic structure millions of years ago are difficult to ignore when dealing with large faceless institutions where there can be little trust and mutuality.

I think we can agree that most current organizations are hierarchies or controlled-access systems. It does not matter whether they are tall or flat or run ruthlessly or compassionately, they are still hierarchies. In such institutions position power reigns. That means that rank, first and foremost, equates to authority instead of expertise.

With rank also comes resource holding power and domination over the behavior and activities of others. As they say, "Rank has its privileges." Regrettably, this does not always mean that people with higher rank are smarter or assume greater responsibility and accountability for the success of an organization and its members. Experience has proven over and over again that strictly "controlled" operations don't necessarily lead to high, sustained levels of productivity. It is also through the exercise of control that the invisible wealth of most ventures remains largely untapped.

In any case, how does self-organization take place in so-called controlled environments? There is no doubt that it takes place since, as I stated before, it is unavoidable and irrepressible. Let's start with the most restricted situations first and then proceed from there to some typical work related examples.

Imagine being locked-up in a gulag, concentration camp, prisoner of war camp or a state prison. Looking from the inside out from any one of these four horrendous places would send a cold chill down anybody's spine. To me they exemplify the ultimate in controlled settings. Consequently, if self-organization is possible in these environments, then it is achievable anywhere.

Although it is difficult to envision, self-organization thrives in these institutions as well as it does anywhere else. If you have a chance ask a person who has survived any of these places of incarceration to tell you in some detail "how" they made it out alive. You will hardly believe what types of prohibited activities have taken place under the strictest forms of surveillance in these penal complexes.

These collaborative actions have included just about everything from tunneling, building airplanes and making uniforms to secret codes, rules of conduct, and individual bravery. Men and women have continued to self-organize even in solitary confinement. Senator John McCain is a great example of a courageous survivor of a prisoner of war camp. He made it home alive from the "Hanoi Hilton" refusing to break even under torture and solitary confinement. He *self*-organized to the very end. The will to survive (part of the common purpose of all living systems) is impossible to extinguish except by death.

Most of today's organizational frameworks are remnants of the Industrial Age. Fundamentally, they are "fine-tuned" hierarchical structures, which have evolved over millennia and, as stated previously, are invariably rank or position power oriented. What I mean by fine-tuned is that engineers in the late 19th century and early 20th century not only designed equipment but in many instances also helped to design organizational structures. Not surprisingly, the governing schemes that they devised were based on a machine metaphor.[5]

What this representation suggests is that an organization, just like a machine, must be constructed from well-defined and precisely assembled interchangeable parts. If these parts fail, for whatever reason, they are simply replaced. Further, these components interact with one another in preset ways specifying the purpose of the assemblage by its configuration.

Hence, control, repair, and reconfiguration are dependent on some type of overall control mechanism or management. Order equates to control and, therefore, a machine or organization is incapable of repairing, reconfiguring, or regenerating itself. Consequently, a business *by design* can't function without a prearranged top down command and control structure. Regrettably, people and social institutions are not machines by any stretch of the imagination.

The effects on people by such public and private systems are not hard to imagine. First, position power or rank unknowingly generates a very powerful but negative atmosphere in *any* of these types of organizations. The reason for this is quite simple. In view of the fact that *intimidation* (perceived or actual and no matter how much or how sparingly used) is the principal instrument employed in running such enterprises, means that their members are kept constantly in a state of psychological tension.[6]

In a controlled-access system every person continuously keeps his or her attention on the center of power. They are poised for instant reaction to the next marketing strategy, bonus plan, restructuring proposal, motivational program or promotion announcements emanating from the "hub" outward. In the meantime, rumors abound with speculations as to what might transpire the following week, month or year. Clearly, such an environment generates relatively high negative emotions and with it narrow thought patterns (since the focus is mainly on individual survival) limiting the sharing of possible potential problems or opportunities that may be developing, not to mention tacit knowledge.

In essence, everyone is persistently trying to determine what the boss or bosses are thinking (mind reading, which is an innate drive) about them and their status in the group. There is perceived "law and order" but the price tag is huge because insecurity is pervasive. Currently United States businesses alone are paying over 300 billion dollars a year for stress related illnesses and that number is steadily increasing.

A brief example from my own life may help to demonstrate how this "tension" permeates in controlled-access institutions and how subtle it can be. I am not known to be neurotic (except to my wife). As a result, for years I was puzzled why there was always a little sense of insecurity as to where I "really" stood in a top down organization. That feeling, I knew, was natural when you are a rookie or when joining a new work group.

However, I have been a member of many entities where, after several years of dedicated service and numerous awards for outstanding accomplishment, I still retained some level of uneasiness as to my fate in the particular institution. That apprehension was distracting and took some of my attention away form more pressing matters. I am sure all of us have similar tales to tell.

The other drawback to hierarchical establishments is the unavoidable self-organization that takes place in these tense and insecure environments. Our motivation for survival is an extremely powerful force that never leaves us until we pass away. Therefore, in order to minimize organizational insecurities, suspicions, reservations about certain procedures and methods of operation, we serendipitously form small mutual support groups and networks. That is the positive side of informal organizations.

Inadvertently, many people, and especially those managers who still believe they can control people, forget that the self-organizing groups can also hinder or even undermine the officially sanctioned programs, as is the case in prisons. That is, individuals will do whatever they think they need to do in order to succeed in life as best as possible. People who feel they have few options available to them may be particularly prone to take some very desperate actions to make ends meet.

Try to recall an occasion from your past work experience when you were a member of a small temporary group composed of representatives from various functional areas. Your assignment was to develop a solution to a pressing problem that was affecting most parts of your organization. You were quite excited that you had been asked to be part of this group. In fact, you had already done some research on the matter and had some preliminary ideas as to how to proceed. Unfortunately, a very self-centered high ranking individual, who already had made up his/her mind about what actions to take, was assigned to supervise the group's activities.

I will speculate that shortly after the first meeting, where most people had "tried" to participate enthusiastically, members of the group started to simply go "through the motions" in trying or attempting to meet the assigned objectives and failed to add much of any significance to the effort. I will also venture to guess that the recommendations that were eventually endorsed by the group were almost identical to what the manager in charge initially proposed. Finally, I'm willing to wager that the solutions to the interdepartmental difficulties (if they were implemented) didn't solve the problems identified, at least not in the long run.

We need to keep in mind that hardly anything gets accomplished in an organization following official rules and regulations to the letter. Primarily, it gets done through the informal networks. The invisible guiding hand (or self-organization) is everywhere where there are people. Human nature can't be circumvented but we keep on trying. Smart enterprises will learn how to leverage the power of these self-organizing groups instead of foolishly ignoring them or even thinking their activities can be controlled.

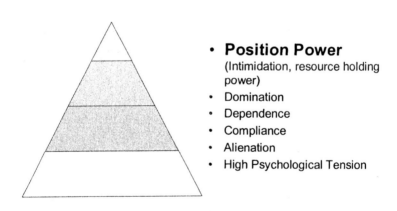

Figure 4-2. Basis for Controlled-Access System Order

Figure 4-2 provides a graphic representation of the basis for order in a controlled-access system. Note that position power, based on intimidation and resource holding power, governs the setting. Focused on control, such an organizational context generates negative order rather than positive order since it's primarily dependent on domination, dependence, and compliance in carrying out its day-to-day activities. As a result, this type of an environment alienates people, creates high levels of psychological tension, and forces informal social networks to function typically in a clandestine mode.

In a shared-access organizational context. A shared-access organizational arrangement by design is an "overt" self-organizing system whose members are not denied access to vital resources by a privileged few or a formally imposed pecking order. What I imply by overt is that the system relies on the *natural informal networks* (also defined as emergent systems) present in all organizations as its primary means of operation. Conversely, in controlled-access environments the informal network is, in effect, pushed "underground" and operates covertly. In a shared-access framework such self-organizing systems are deliberately elevated to the center stage as much as possible.

The informal groups become the core operational elements by having the opportunity to continuously buy-in and help up-date the common vision and mission of the enterprise as a whole as well as partaking in the day-to-day activities. Hence, every member of a venture becomes a partner insuring that individual as well as organizational goals are quite evenly matched. Everyone is responsible and accountable for helping to manage the critical resources. That really is the only way we can tap into the powerful dynamics of the invisible assets present in every social group.

We know these informal networks influence the performance of groups as much as or more than the formally established processes, including orders issued from the highest levels of an organization. We also have learned, through extensive research, that these emergent systems may support or oppose, supplement or sabotage what is formally required. It all depends on the work environment. Thus, if we can't circumvent human nature then why not take full advantage of it?

In brief, organizations run by *unmanagement* are, in effect, systems composed of highly interconnected parallel-operating networks composed of self-reliant autonomous members and free flowing teams. These autonomous elements are kept on course not by a top down command and control structure, but by a common identity that maintains *dynamic order* (see model in Chapter Seven). The system spawns positive emotions and thereby stimulates more expansive and resourceful thinking, not to mention greater sharing of tacit knowledge. It also feeds on itself and in so doing generates new ideas exponentially.

Further, because the components of the enterprise are comparatively autonomous, they are by design not precisely configured or connected to one another in static pre-established ways. As a consequence, these elements react independently based on the circumstances of their immediate surroundings and the needs of the entire organization. Such a system is extremely reactive, capable of responding to changing conditions instantly without the necessity of external direction and control.

Shared-access endeavors are by no means perfect but they certainly are a much better alternative for success in the Knowledge Age than its counterparts, the controlled-access organizations. The overt self-organizing systems also are frameworks in which, given the choice, all humans would prefer to live for obvious evolutionary reasons. It is in these types of social settings where the best qualities of our kind have an opportunity to flourish such as the arts and sciences. Evolution has given us the capacity to be exceptionally complex and egalitarian social creatures given the right conditions.

Think of a "real" collaborative experience you've had in the past or maybe recently and recall the "invisible energy" that emerged during that occasion. Let's say it was another interdisciplinary team that was formed to solve a company-wide problem. In this case, however, there was no manager assigned to run the show. Instead, the individual or individuals who identified the predicament solicited for volunteers from all areas of the firm to form a team in order to find a long term solution to the problem. Once the team was formed its leadership was shared and situational (discussed in the next chapter). In a relatively short time an innovative and practical solution emerged and was quickly implemented with the assistance of the team members throughout the organization.

Is the above example a "pipe dream?" Not by a long shot and I'm convinced that most of you have had similar experiences. Can you imagine an entire organization functioning like that? If you can, then you have visualized precisely how a shared-access system like W. L. Gore and Associates (described in more detail at the end of the next chapter) operates. It's a powerful framework that thrives without bosses.

The illustration above is from an actual case brought to my attention recently by one of my MBA students. Sadly, it ended on a negative note when one of the senior managers of the firm eventually noticed the tremendous success that the team of volunteers was having. Without delay he appointed himself team leader and the group disbanded within two weeks. It's a classic example of why informal networks can't be controlled.

Are there other organizations besides W. L. Gore and Associates currently in existence that fit the shared-access mold? Yes, there are and the numbers are growing as we discover more and more about the significance of self-organizing systems and the types of organizational contexts that are best suited for humans instead of machines. Companies that can be included on this list are IDEO, Rowe Furniture, Koch Industries, Great Harvest Bread, the computer software firm SAS, and Semco in Brazil.

IDEO, for instance, is the world's leading product design company. Therefore, it is almost exclusively reliant on the continuous generation of new innovative product designs for other enterprises from tooth brushes to medical equipment and computer screens. Not surprisingly, it operates in a shared-access mode where there is no rank or position power and people work in free flowing teams where tacit knowledge is shared unreservedly. Undoubtedly, IDEO couldn't be as successful as it is functioning in a controlled-access configuration.

- **Expert Power** (Attraction, social attention holding potential)
- Collaboration
- Interdependence
- Commitment
- Satisfaction
- Low Psychological Tension

Figure 4-3. Basis for Shared-Access System Order

Figure 4-3 summarizes the basis for order in a shared-access system. As can be seen, expert power, centered on personal attraction and social attention holding potential, is the primary energizing force of such a framework. Thus, the system fosters voluntary collaboration, interdependence, and individual commitment. It's an environment where people's innate drives have an opportunity to be expressed in a balanced fashion resulting in high levels of personal satisfaction and low overall psychological tension. Clearly, this type of a setting allows informal social networks to operate as overtly as possible and, in the process, spawns positive rather than negative order.

3.   SOCIAL NESTING

So, what does all that we have discussed in this chapter add up to? The straightforward answer is, *social capital.* Without ample "quantities" of social capital not much in the way of productive work, and especially new knowledge generation, takes place in an organization.

I like to portray social capital also as social nesting. In my opinion a community or clan, if it is to function as a closely-knit group, must first develop an inordinate array of positive personal ties among its members. Therefore, an organization must first build its own distinctive "nest" where its constituents are able to interact comfortably with each other without any reservations. Remember that few things in organizations are accomplished by strictly following formal directives. Hence, without enough social capital an enterprise is, for all intents and purposes, merely a collection of employees or hired hands waiting for instructions from the bosses.

One of the most current and meaningful definitions of social capital that I have found reads as follows:

> Social capital is the goodwill available to individuals or groups. Its source lies in the structure and content of the actor's social relations. Its effects flow from the information, influence, and solidarity it makes available to the actor [or actors].[7]

In essence, social capital is based on the trusting and mutual relationships formed by people over time. It is composed of tightly composed support networks that provide the information, influential connections, and camaraderie needed by all of us for meaningful existence. It is also something that can't be managed or controlled. Social capital is the very foundation of *voluntary* interdependent associations. It develops through circular causality and self-organization as opposed to top down directives and position power.

One can now see that the more social capital an organization is able to develop, the more it can accomplish things that others can only dream about. It also now becomes apparent why there is such a critical relationship between social capital, self-organization, and the emergence and exchange of tacit knowledge. This closely knit association among the triad of organizational success factors will become increasingly apparent as we continue our quest for invisible wealth.

Social nesting is, above all, about people fully realizing that they are vital members of an internal and external network of mutually supporting connections. As one can readily surmise, these networks are exceptionally dependent on *reciprocity*. This means that the individuals involved must be concerned with the well being of others, as well as their own, in striving to help build an organizational framework founded on empathy and trust. Clearly, highly developed and institutionally supportive social capital networks are almost impossible to develop and sustain in groups of more than 150 members.

This by no means is intended to infer that challenges and disagreements should be discouraged in developing and maintaining social capital. In fact, the opposite is true. In an institution with a rich social capital base new ideas and innovations are *expected* to be closely scrutinized by the network members but in an atmosphere of trust and without attacking people personally. Challenges and disagreements are fundamental in assuring organizational vitality and success.

Incessant *voluntary collaboration* or social capital is the most important element for any organization, particularly those that are knowledge based. The reason for that is fairly obvious. Social nesting is an invisible yet extremely powerful organizational component that can't be duplicated by potential competitors. Every institution is composed of different individuals and a dissimilar collective "chemistry" that is self-sustaining and mutually reinforcing. Consequently, even if two businesses are roughly the same size and produce an identical product they can never develop the same type and quality of social capital.

Social capital is founded on many interrelated dimensions. One, as mentioned earlier, is size. In a large institution the nesting usually is relatively "shallow" providing little or negligible support for formal efforts. Thus, it is best that these organizations be composed of small semi-autonomous "clans" each working around a core-competency but at the same time tightly coupled to other similar groups.

How a business is organized is another dimension that requires attention. For example, what types of relationships are possible, and through what process, is central to the development of social capital. In a controlled-access system or hierarchy there may be various channels that are difficult, if not impossible, for many people to gain entry to.

For instance, many people in the "front lines" seldom gain access to, or they may be reluctant to, contact higher levels of management. Naturally, the reverse is also true. In such cases important connections may never be developed or are by-passed or ignored. That can present dire consequences for an organization.

What types of relationships people develop is another important dimension. Namely, how all embracing are the friendships that influence people's behavior? That, of course, includes the amount of respect and prestige network members receive or give to each other. Finally, members of a group who have high levels of social capital need to have some form of shared identity. This includes relatively common values, task interpretations, and worldviews in general. I will discuss this in more detail in the next chapter.

One of the most significant points to remember is that *the more self-organization is practiced **openly**, instead of being pushed underground, the more social capital an institution will generate.* The opposite is also true. The more structure and controls are imposed on an organization, by either formal directives or direct supervision, the more the informal system will become covert and dispersed. Moreover, it may over time begin to undermine, rather than support, formal objectives. The worst examples of this, of course, are the secretive social organizations found in every prison. One can now see why it makes little sense for any organization to try to circumvent human nature and self-organization by relying on ever tighter controls but many keep on trying.

Also, contrasting other forms of assets, social capital is owned mutually by the members of a network and can't be simply traded or sold as other assets. Hence, no single party has exclusive rights to it, although it is the single most powerful dimension of an organization, which allows it to accomplish the impossible when the social nesting is well developed.[8]

Mergers provide a classic example of the vital importance of social capital and why overlooking this invisible asset can have serious consequences for such endeavors. As we all are aware, mergers and acquisitions have become extremely popular in the past couple of decades for leveraging combined organizational assets as evidenced by their ever-increasing numbers. With the exception of occasional business down turns, I am sure they will continue at about the same or higher pace in the future. What is most startling about these mergers and acquisitions is that about 80 percent of them fail to create any of the expected benefits for the parties involved. Worse yet, roughly 50 percent of the amalgamations actually decrease their combined values.

What is even more amazing is that these proceedings are not undertaken without considerable time and effort spent on analysis and negotiations. Also, because these endeavors are complex, they are hardly ever conducted without the involvement of scores of seasoned experts in the field. In addition, countless books have been written on the subject and many universities offer courses on mergers and acquisitions.[9]

So, why do most mergers and acquisitions fail, especially when the topic has been so well researched? The answers to this question from numerous experts run the gamut from lack of clear strategy and incompatible cultures to shortsighted reward systems and insufficient communications. I suggest that these are only the symptoms of the problem and don't include the real underlying causes. Instead, it's my contention that the actual reasons for these failures are twofold. They include the vast disengagements of two well developed systems of informal networks and the depreciation of social capital that gave each of the merging organizations their real *sustainable* value in the first place.

For instance, mergers and acquisitions have great difficulty including anything other than what is in the financial records in the analysis process. Consequently, there is no way to account for the intangibles such as the tacit knowledge that resides in the minds of organizational members *and* all the intricate informal connections and networks that have been carefully honed over the years. Thus, what appears on the ledgers under "intellectual capital" (trademarks, patents, documented services or manufacturing processes, and so on) accounts for less than half of what that vital asset is actually worth.

As a result, when a merger takes place and a new organization is assembled, there are usually no provisions to retain the value of the intangibles that are the real foundation for the intellectual assets displayed on the books. No matter how few people, if any, are let go most of the critical networks and their connections are at least partially severed and no provisions are in place to help establish new ones as quickly as possible.

Even under the best of circumstances it takes time for people to make new connections and there are no guarantees what the results will be. It is a self-organizing process that can't be managed. Cisco is one of the few companies that is well aware of the merger paradox and takes special precautions to limit the loss of the real knowledge base in their acquisitions.[10]

We can now begin to appreciate the negative consequences of attempting to control people and designing social systems using a machine metaphor as a guide. Thus, although not perfect, the shared-access organizational framework is best suited for human beings. In the next chapter I will begin to combine what I have presented so far to demonstrate what can be systematically done to unleash the incredible hidden power of the informal groups and networks that inhabit every social system.

Chapter 5

UNLEASHING THE INFORMAL NETWORKS

Few people question the fact that at least the developed countries of the world have long passed the doorstep of the information dependent Knowledge Age. Yet ironically, most institutions are still governed by, albeit refined, Industrial Age governing frameworks based on a machine metaphor. Yes, we've "flattened" many of our organizations in a variety of fields but unfortunately, flat or tall, they still are controlled-access or hierarchical systems. Such entities simply are not very effective in fostering high levels of voluntary collaboration among knowledge professionals necessary for sustained intellectual capital generation.

Thus, we need to completely rethink how we can increase the productivity of knowledge workers in their quest for new innovative products and services. Autonomy (tempered with responsibility and accountability), reciprocity, and interdependence should be the major features of a new Knowledge Age mode of resource attainment and distribution. I believe that can best be accomplished within the framework of a *shared-access system* that facilitates the unleashing of the invisible power of informal networks. Overt, as opposed to covert, self-organization is the foundation of a shared-access system and the focus of this chapter.

So far we have examined the longitudinal societal success factors of our hunter-gatherer ancestors, determined that people can't be controlled, and concluded that social capital is all about voluntary interdependent connections between individuals. Now it's time to begin to combine these major building blocks into a coherent framework that today's organizations can put to practical use.

1.   ORGANIZATIONAL MEMBERSHIP

True, any assemblages of individuals will self-organize themselves into some kind of dynamic order depending on the circumstances and the characteristics of the people involved. The resultant dynamic order, however, may or may not support the intended goals of the formal organization. It may even undermine or sabotage the officially required activities and behavioral norms. In essence, it may produce negative dynamic order.

In order to leverage the power of informal networks *productively*, one needs to promote positive or aligned dynamic order (see Figure 7-2). Only the right mix of people, who are capable of developing and maintaining a shared identity, can realistically achieve that end. Accordingly, I will begin this chapter by first outlining the general desired profile and the selection process of shared-access systems' associates.

Please keep in mind that "associates" in a shared-access system are inherently partners. Hence, they have nothing in common with the people called associates in such companies as Wal-Mart who are simply employees by another name. Sadly, calling employees associates without also giving them the appropriate responsibility and accountability in helping to run an enterprise only increases their cynicism and hardly ever increases their motivation to perform at higher levels. "Employees" are seldom, if ever, misled by meaningless position titles.

As briefly suggested in Chapter Two, for today's organizations to gain the full self-organizing benefits of their informal small groups they have to be very selective as to who is asked to join the *clan* (a clan portrays a closer relationship among its members than a group, firm or organization). Remember that the hunter-gatherer groups were composed of close relatives and friends. Thus, in putting together a small and very collaborative work group, one must not only assure that its members have the required talent and skills, but that they have the abilities to form close ties. Without such ties people's altruistic tendencies will have difficulty in having an opportunity to be expressed.

Considerable research in the past two decades has shown that cooperation among people is fundamentally dependent on two aspects; how much members of a given group care about the future and how they perceive their actions affecting the decisions of other associates. As Duncan J. Watts stipulates:

> Only if the future matters can the prospect of doing unto others make a short-term sacrifice seem worthwhile. Caring about the future, however, is not enough. Only if you believe that by supporting the collective

interest you will cause others to join you, does the future give you any selfish incentive to do so. And the only way you can assess how much of a difference you can make, and whether it will be enough, is if you pay attention to the actions of others. If it looks like enough people are joining in, you may decide that it is worth joining in also. If not you won't. As a consequence, the decision of whether or not to cooperate depends critically on what we call *coordination externalities*.[1]

That is precisely why I believe so strongly that the specific *context* of an organization is so vital for the development and maintenance of voluntary cooperation and the generation of new knowledge. I'll discuss this more later in the chapter.

For that reason finding and retaining first-rate people that "fit" into a shared-access endeavor is essential for four major reasons. First, you are literally searching for "new family members" or partners, not just for employees who can perform certain tasks, because you want to assure that both sides of human nature have a chance of being expressed in a balanced manner. That can only take place among close friends. "Employees" are mercenaries who normally run to the highest bidders. Partners, on the other hand, are part owners whose welfare depends on the present and future success of an organization.

Second, you want people who have a long-term interest in your organization. Retention of members is vital. Without wide-ranging relationships and close cooperation, which take considerable time to evolve, high levels of social capital are impossible to develop and maintain. A controlled-access system is much better suited for enterprises where turnover is relatively high and there is little desire to make changes that would increase retention.

Third, you want to find people who have certain talents that would have a major positive impact on the success of a company. Thus, in the screening process you have to differentiate between an individual's talents, knowledge, and skills.[2] Talents are similar to innate drives in that they are genetically based. If that was not the case everybody could become a great painter, test pilot or super athlete. All they would have to do is practice, practice, practice.

We can acquire a wealth of knowledge through education and practical experiences. We can also learn certain skills like operating a machine or using a computer language. Unfortunately, we cannot acquire a talent since it is inherited. We can only strengthen our talents through frequent use once we have discovered what they are. Therefore, we must look for people who have identified their talents and, just as importantly, know how to apply those abilities effectively.

Finally, you need to invite people to join the clan who are mentally stable, open-minded, self-reliant, highly motivated, and conscientious. At the same time they must be willing to work in teams when that is appropriate. They should also be ready to take full responsibility and accountability for the successes and failures of the organization as a whole. You expect that from partners. In effect, you want to attract *self-motivated people,* since in a shared-access system there are no managers who are responsible for bossing and "motivating" the employees.

This doesn't mean that the individuals we are recruiting ought to be "clones" with whom we have little difficulty socializing. As alluded to earlier, "yes people" and linear thinkers need not apply. Diversity, challenges, and disagreements are central to the functioning of a shared-access system, which is dependent on extensive voluntary sharing of tacit knowledge. However, this exchange of multiple ideas takes place in an environment of trust where everyone knows they will be fully heard and that their views will be respected even though they are not always accepted.

Further, I am not overly enthusiastic about using an array of instruments to help screen people in the selection process. If certain instruments are used, such as the Big Five Personality Test ("...the five-factor model clearly denotes that there are stable individual differences in the degree to which people are naturally collaborative [that is, extroverted] and trusting [that is, agreeable."][3], they should not be the primary means to evaluate candidates. Instruments can't verify matching "chemistry." Rather, numerous personal interviews and meetings should be used to determine who would be invited to join the organization. In fact, for the benefit of all concerned, potential associates should be, when possible, asked to temporarily work in their future surroundings for a week or two.

Essentially, there should be ample opportunity for people to determine if there *appears* to be a good fit (there is no perfect way to make that determination) between the clan and the applicant. Conversely, the contender should be provided sufficient occasions to decide if they are truly comfortable and interested in the offer to join the firm. W. L. Gore and Associates, for instance, may interview prospective candidates as many as 10 to 12 times. They must have a valid reason for relying on such a far-reaching process, having operated successfully in a shared-access mode since 1958.

Many companies frown on conducting extensive interviews with candidates, not to mention multiple appointments and trial runs, because of the expense. Yes, far-reaching engagements with prospective members are expensive, but usually the payoff in the long run is much greater than the initial costs incurred.

A brief example should further clarify the significance of devoting sufficient time and effort to the selection process. A good friend of mine, whose very successful "hobby" for the past couple of decades has been to turn around small and medium sized companies, currently is the CEO of an undersized software firm that he took over a couple of years ago. The downsized staff of the company seems to be quite knowledgeable and talented. Regrettably, because most of them appear to have little awareness of their specific talents, they are unable put them to practical use.

This small group is also fairly sociable with no apparent animosity between any of its members. Although everyone is on friendly terms, they have considerable difficulty in working as a team. That seems to be their biggest obstacle in integrating their talents and effectively pursuing organizational goals. Not knowing how to function as a team isn't an uncommon predicament in many companies. The irony is that the CEO has, from day one, tried to educate and coach the staff in how to function as an effective team and has even occasionally sought the help of external consultants.

"Hypothetically" the small workforce is relatively familiar with the fundamental differences between groups and teams. For instance, they know that teams have both individual and mutual accountability, whereas group members have primarily individual accountability; that in effective teams decisions are made by consensus, objectives are well understood and accepted, free expression of ideas is expected, roles are clear and mutually supported, and leadership is shared. Conversely, the staff is aware that groups have majority and minority opinions, criticism tends to be destructive (that is why it is usually avoided), common objectives may not be thoroughly accepted, personal feelings are typically hidden, and people tend to protect their turf.

The above idiosyncrasies of groups are directly applicable to this small software firm. To be exact, most of the group members are unwilling to take the lead in solving a problems or pursuing opportunities. They seem unable to assume responsibility and accountability for their actions. Worse, when commitments and deadlines are not met, no one is willing to confront those individuals who missed their assignments for fear of offending them. In addition, people avoid bringing up these issues during meetings. Fundamentally, these folks want someone else (the CEO) to tell them what to do and to take responsibility for those actions.

Has the CEO been derelict in his duties? Hardly. As mentioned before, he has placed major emphasis on education and training. He also gives more than ample opportunities to individuals for improving their performance. In fact, several members of his staff have personally verified to me that the problems mentioned above are indeed hampering their efforts. These folks are unmistakably "frozen" in their ways of thinking and behaving and, thus, are unable to adjust to the changed work context.

Again, change is both cognitive and physiological. Simply put, most members of this company have expressed some of their self-centered genetic predispositions so frequently (recall the thickness of the arrows in Figure 3-1) that it is almost impossible for them to express their other-centered drives even when the conditions have changed. Therefore, the CEO has no alternative but to begin looking for people who are more self-reliant and willing to work in an overt self-organizing environment. Based on his past successes with unmanagement, he certainly isn't about to run the company in a typical controlled-access mode.

2.   PRINCIPLES SUPPORTING OVERT SELF-ORGANIZATION

Having established in Chapter Three that our innate drives are the core of the self-organizing process, and emphasized the need for devoting considerable time and effort to member selection, we can now examine the substance and dynamic relationships of the four fundamental principles governing "overt" self-organization (see Figure 5-1). We must keep in mind that these vital elements are the backbone for *leveraging the constructive power* of the informal collaborative networks residing within all groups. They are also the key for the development of social contexts that facilitate the balanced expression of our genetic predispositions.

However, before I discuss the details of my model it's necessary that I first substantiate the deep-seated significance of the four key self-organizing principles. Simply put, before someone is willing to adopt a new concept they need to be convinced, as much as possible, that it makes practical sense. Therefore, I will briefly revisit the major long-term societal success factors of the hunter-gatherers discussed earlier and review three more recently validated theoretical constructs that support the validity of the interconnected principles that I advocate.

Recall the following five primary success factors of the foragers that were identified:
- Lived in relatively small very interdependent groups composed of kin and close friends.
- Maintained high sustained levels of reciprocity, egalitarianism, and practiced consensus decision-making.
- Members owned their own means of production.
- Respected individual autonomy and self-reliance tempered with high social responsibility and accountability.

- Practiced situational or shared leadership based on expertise (social attention holding power) rather than rank (resource holding power) and there were no status differences between the sexes.

What stands out in the scrutiny of the five factors above is that for hundreds of millennia our kind maintained fluid social structures where the self-organizing process was as overt as possible and, as a result, the levels of social capital were also high. Yet again, the more self-organizing is practiced openly, instead of being pushed "underground", the more social capital a group will have to support its primary goals and objectives. That is the essence of unmanagement and its reinforcing flexible structure, the shared-access system. Hence, the success factors of our hunter-gatherer ancestors have been fully incorporated into the model.

The overt self-organizing principles of the hunter-gatherers have also been recently validated by the identification of critical elements required for small groups to be able to self-organize and by chaos and complexity theories. For instance, the presence of four key elements has been found to support self-organization in small groups. First, there needs to be sufficient periphery openness (interaction with the immediate environment), an investigational aptitude (willingness to learn), attentiveness to deep common vision and values (individual self-reference), and lastly, a capacity to move as a whole (shared identity), adjusting to changing conditions as necessary.[4] These elements certainly add to the credence of the hunter-gatherer success factor.

Further, the self-organizing principles of our ancestors are also supported by the basic tenets of chaos and complexity theories.[5] Chaos theory stipulates that a system (person or group) is unpredictable and bounded at the same time. Hence, such a configuration never attains true equilibrium since it is very sensitive to small disturbances all the time or is never precisely in the same place twice. Concurrently, the system never goes beyond certain margins. It has a self-reference to which it ceaselessly returns. For example, every person's behavior is never exactly the same but, simultaneously, it's bounded by his or her unique personality and physical traits. Also, in a self-organizing group, individual autonomy is tempered by social responsibility and accountability.

Complexity theory holds that non-linear and unpredictable systems (people and groups) are more complex than linear, cyclical, and predictable structures like machines and controlled-access systems. Furthermore, disequilibria are a necessary condition for growth. Therefore, as a system becomes unstable amid turbulence, it's then able to restructure into a configuration that exhibits more viable properties than previously.

Thus, efforts to use linear and predictable mechanisms to control non-linear frameworks make little sense. The message for today's organizations (and, of course, this was also applicable to the hunter-gatherers) is that since they must interact with a constantly changing, information-rich and complex environment, they must be equally multifaceted and flexible in order to survive. It's quite apparent why structures founded on a machine metaphor have an adverse affect on complex organic beings, such as humans.

In view of the above, I have taken the five critical success factors of the hunter-gatherers, in addition to the other supportive theories assessed, and incorporated them into an integrated practical framework that can be used by any organization to increase their social capital levels and sharing of tacit knowledge. Figure 5-1 exhibits the four fundamental *integrated principles* supporting overt self-organization that help cultivate and strengthen the positive elements of the invisible guiding hand (the balanced expression of innate human drives) at the center of the model.

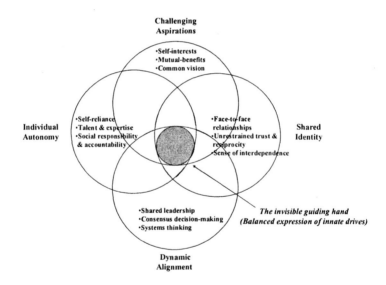

Figure 5-1. Principles Supporting Overt Self-Organization

The most important aspect regarding the model that needs to be kept in mind as we progress through its basic elements, and as we later begin to apply it, is that it is dynamic and interdependent. In effect, it is a parallel operating system where all of its components function together simultaneously. Thus, an overt self-organizing system works best when the requirements of each principle have been fully developed so that the innate drives of its members can be expressed in a balanced manner.

Individual autonomy. It's most appropriate to begin the exploration of the essential precepts of overt self-organizing systems with the primary underpinnings of any social group, the individual. We have already looked at the necessity of being extremely selective in determining who should be asked to join the clan. Being very selective has nothing to do with being arrogant or "snobbish." Every organization needs to screen people one way or another to at least assure they hire people who have the skills to fill an institutional void.

The bottom line is that *it is not easy to work in a shared-access environment*. Individuals who have become accustomed to functioning in "8 to 5" or controlled-access settings have great difficulty in accepting the high levels of personal responsibility and accountability that an open self-organizing system demands. There is no place for "hired hands" in a shared-access arrangement because there are no bosses to issue directives or "employees" to carry them out. Rather, the system is comprised of partners or associates whose activities and interactions are founded on personal commitments and not on compliance with orders.

Therefore, for positive self-organization (as opposed to the underground type which can be meagerly positive, neutral or negative) to take place a clan needs to be composed of self-reliant people able and willing to function, both independently and in multiple teams, depending on the circumstances. A partnership demands that each affiliate contribute something valuable to a venture. Hence, a shared-access organization functions on the synergy of its combined resources (human and otherwise), hard work, and perseverance of the people involved. There are no entitlements, only rewards and satisfaction from results achieved.

Clearly, this means that people must know what their abilities and proficiencies are (their means of production) and, above all, how to effectively apply them on their own or in concert with other people. After all, the underpinnings of the power of the invisible organizational success factors are the combined talents and efforts applied willingly by its members.

Finally, the need for individual autonomy in an overt self-organizing system is counter balanced by the necessity that members also be highly socially responsible and accountable. There is no place for "Rambos" or hermits, but that does not suggest that members need to be party animals. Instead, what a shared-access establishment does require is that people not only assume responsibility and accountability for their actions, but also for the activities of the *entire organization*.

As one can imagine, that is easier said than done. For instance, in our society when something goes wrong, usually everybody immediately looks for a "scapegoat" and, at the same time, people distance themselves from the problem for fear of being targeted as the guilty party. In a genuine partnership, however, everyone takes credit or assumes fault no matter what transpires. That is the ultimate sign of a true mutually supportive relationship where our other-centered innate drives have the greatest chance of being expressed. Not every person is capable or willing to assume total answerability for a group's activities.

In persistent voluntary relationships all parties concerned are very dependent on two interrelated qualities—interdependence and reciprocity—as was the case with the hunter-gatherers. Wise self-reliant individuals have learned that autonomy needs to be tempered with interdependence where one acknowledges that helping others to grow also has a helpful impact on the mentor. Moreover, that means being the enabler in one case and willing to become the apprentice in another as conditions warrant.[6]

Additionally, valid partnerships are dependent on reciprocity. This, of course, connotes that ideas and other resources are readily shared for mutual benefits. As importantly, all members must also be ready and able to assume both leadership and follower roles as conditions change. Remember, leadership in the shared-access context has absolutely nothing to do with "position power" but instead is based on expertise and the willingness to distribute that know-how widely. I will discuss shared leadership in detail in the next chapter.

Thus, as the need for a particular expertise or talent changes from one problem or opportunity to the next, so does the acceptance and assumption of leadership. As we well know, many people are very uncomfortable in filling both positions. They are much more accustomed to permanently filling one of the two roles instead of alternating between them. Credit the Industrial Age mind-set for that. In an open self-organizing system, however, there is no place for position power, but there are all kinds of opportunities for volunteers willing to take the lead under the right conditions.

Shared identity. Every close-knit social entity, akin to a family, has a very unique shared identity or special chemistry that, like glue, holds it together through good times and bad. A clan is a distinctive living and breathing biological system with its own needs and goals as it tries to survive as best as possible in its particular environment.

This shared identity is distinctive for two reasons. First, as far as we know, no two people born onto our planet have ever been entirely identical.

This will be true even if or when we "attempt" to clone individuals. Recollect, we are all self-organizing beings down to our DNA molecules. As a result, it is impossible to clone completely indistinguishable biological forms. We can come close to creating "earthlings" very similar to identical twins (who are never really identical) but they will never be an exact copy of someone else as long as the process remains biological. Thus, each group is made up of distinctive members. That alone makes each social body different from another.

Second, after a group is formed it begins to develop unique voluntary connections between its constituents as the members seek to pursue their perceived survival options (self-organize) within the assemblage. Clearly, the more open this process is and remains, the more constructive and group specific these networks become throughout the enterprise. Also, over time these connections become more supportive and intense. Of course, that gives the innate drives of the people involved a continuous "workout" in a balanced fashion eventually making their expressions more deep-seated and forceful as illustrated by Figure 5-1. According to Watts:

> All the things we do, all the features that define us, and all the activities we pursue that lead us to meet and interact with each other are contexts. So the set of contexts in which each of us participates is an extremely important determinant of the network structure that we subsequently create.[7]

Consequently, the unique set of people and the connections that evolve between them produces the distinctive chemistry or shared identity within a clan that only they can put to productive use. Equally important, that uniqueness can't be fully emulated by another social entity no matter how they might try. That certainly gives an organization a competitive advantage.

Nonetheless, I need to add a cautionary note. Although enterprises, like people, can't be wholly cloned, there are thousands of companies that try to do exactly that encouraged along by hordes of consultants. Ironically, the same is true at the individual level where people are constantly barraged by hundreds of different advertisements for diets and fitness routines, each claiming that theirs is the perfect regimen. There is nothing wrong with learning from the "best practices" of successful institutions and people as long as we understand that no organization or individual can perform exactly in the same manner (even if they are in a similar industry or field) as another. With biological systems one size doesn't fit all!

Institutions can use precisely the same types of equipment but when it comes to people the similarities fade rapidly. That is why *the principles of self-organization I am advocating for accessing the invisible triad of organizational success factors are not prescriptive but descriptive.* What this means is that every venture wishing to take advantage of these principles must apply them in their own matchless way.

More precisely, each social group needs to incorporate the model into their own distinctive chemistry. Experts can help in examining the intricacies of the principles and what they do or do not represent. Nevertheless, the arduous work of discovering what needs to be done and actually how it will be carried out can only be brought to fruition by the *combined efforts* of the clan members themselves. How else can overt self-organization be initiated and sustained?

Also, bear in mind that humans are physiologically incapable of establishing relatively close ties with more than about 150 people. Therefore, overt self-organization systems can only be realistically nurtured within groups with 150 or less members. In larger clusters relationships become fragmented, ties of common interest can't be effectively maintained, and hierarchies creep in. In effect, within more sizable groups overall close social ties weaken or disappear becoming confined to small separate cliques and various formalized "control" systems slowly begin to take shape.

Thus, a strong sense of interdependence can only be developed in an environment that is small enough where everyone can maintain face-to-face or line-of-sight relationships with all group members. The best indicator that people are maintaining excellent face-to-face interactions is when everybody in an organization is able to greet each person by their first names. Therefore, in order to facilitate the development of close ties and the emergence of a deep-rooted shared identity, organizational size must be limited to around 150 people.

I personally recommend restricting membership to roughly 30 to 100 individuals whenever possible in order to attain the utmost benefits from overt self-organization and to make equitable handling of financial rewards among partners less complicated. For instance, if everyone is a partner then owning less than one percent of the shares of an enterprise starts to become meaningless (see Chapter Six for more details).

Bear in mind that hunter-gatherer bands seldom were composed of more than 30 to 50 constituents. Also, remember that large enterprises can be partitioned into small comparatively autonomous groups (organized around certain core competencies) and tightly networked with one another through a common vision, information technology, financial systems and other linkages.

Limiting the size of organizations or their components is the easy part. By enhancing face-to-face contact it will probably generate some of the physiological changes (hormone levels and neurotransmitter activity) discussed previously, which are necessary for effective interpersonal communications and relationships. It may also reduce the chances for violence among the members.

Small size alone, however, will fall short of facilitating the emergence of a truly evocative shared identity essential for sustaining significant levels of social capital. One of the most effective ways of developing unrestrained trust, a sense of interdependence among people, and increase the robustness of the shared identity within an organization is through teams. Hence, "real teams" accomplish most work in a shared-access environment, although much is also achieved through individual efforts when that is the most suitable option.

Real teams are composed of *volunteers* since in an open self-organizing system no one makes assignments for someone else. People make their own commitments and their reputations depend on how well they keep those obligations. Team membership should be quite diverse including a suitable mix of abilities, skills, and experiences. Each individual needs to be well versed regarding group dynamics, and each team should fully manage their own activities. People should also be free to join several teams as long as they are able to fulfill their commitments to each team. Finally, every team needs to keep abreast of what other teams throughout the enterprise are doing to assure that all team activities are fully coordinated for the benefit of the organization as a whole.

Close face-to-face relationships and teams don't only help to develop strong common ties but also bring about mutually beneficial growth and the sharing of tacit knowledge that occurs when people interact voluntarily. In real teams members develop a sense of responsibility and a desire to be both teachers and learners. As we are well aware, learning is most effective when we have an open and supportive forum where new ideas can be presented so that they can be fully examined, challenged and improved upon before they are applied. Such frank discussions take place only in an organizational context where there is unrestrained reciprocity, high levels of trust, and mutual respect for others.

Challenging aspirations. An open self-organizing system is fully dependent on mutually supportive processes that allow it to function with voluntary cooperation without the need of a formalized structure and management controls. For that reason, the third integrated principle provides the framework, an internal compass that helps to keep all its members and teams advancing towards common objectives without the necessity for conventional policies and directives.

Goals must give organizational affiliates much more than direction. They not only have to be challenging but also inspiring. Most institutions have difficult targets but seldom do they motivate people to reach for greater heights. For instance, a goal of increasing sales by twenty percent for next year will not get anybody very excited. Genuine common intentions must take into consideration members' feelings, hopes, and aspirations; otherwise they are not very meaningful. Thus, for example, a goal of eradicating a certain disease in ten years for the benefit of all humankind is much more thought provoking.

Bear in mind how well all the members of hunter-gatherer clans knew where they had been, what needed to be accomplished at the moment, and where they wanted to go next. There were no secrets and decisions were made by consensus. The same principles are applicable today, if we want self-organization to be practiced openly instead of covertly. Therefore, in a shared-access, system defining challenging and aspiring goals is a never-ending dynamic process involving all associates where the focus is on both self-interest and mutual benefits. The outcome of this continuous interdependent process is a *living document* called the common vision. It's the foundation for a clan's mutually beneficial *challenging aspirations* (see Appendix A for an example of a common vision).

Being truly open about personal interests, goals and values is difficult practice at best. Defining shared values and mutually beneficial options to pursue is an even more gut-wrenching process, to say the least. Yet both practices are vital for supporting overt self-organization by providing it dynamic aspiring direction. Consequently, since a common vision is such a vital document, considerable time and effort need to be devoted to its development and maintenance. In fact, the process of putting the common vision together and getting total buy-in from all clan members is at least as essential as the final product, which in reality never is final.

Also, all members of a shared-access system must periodically review the common vision to assure that it is still up-to-date as well as sufficiently challenging and aspiring. As we well know, undemanding and uninspiring goals are especially detrimental to any sort of voluntary collaboration. Hence, whether working alone or in a team(s), each affiliate should always be concerned and motivated to accomplish whatever is required both in the short- and long-run to constantly further the success of the organization.

Furthermore, new members joining the clan need to have ample opportunity to absorb the contents of the common vision and be able to ask relevant questions before they are able to adopt it for their own use. New associates, however, should not be permitted to make significant changes to the document until they have gained sufficient experience in the activities of the venture.

The principle of challenging aspirations is about developing goals that can satisfy both individual self-interests and mutual-interests without one impeding the attainment of the other. It is a delicate balancing act but well worth the effort. As is the case with all the principles, there is nothing mechanical or routine about the cultivation and maintenance of a common vision. It is a dynamic serendipitous process that at times seems "messy" and redundant but its powerful influence is more than worth the effort. Without a true common vision and the continuous involvement of motivated people an organization is essentially adrift.

Dynamic alignment. Like sailing ships at sea, people and organizations occasionally get off course or even begin to drift aimlessly. When that occurs, the person or persons who first become aware of the anomaly need to immediately sound the alarm and alert the rest of the crew of the situation so that appropriate action can be taken without delay.

In a shared-access environment, there is no captain nor are there mates to make major decisions and to issue orders. Rather, every member of the ship must be ready and willing to take the helm when a fitting moment presents itself. They must also be willing to follow when that is the best option. Accordingly, dynamic alignment is all about shared or situational leadership, consensus decision-making, systems thinking, and individual commitment. The entire next chapter is devoted to this subject so I will be brief in describing the intricacies of the fourth principle of an open self-organizing system.

As I have alluded, every constituent of a self-organizing system should be prepared and willing to assume a leadership role depending on the problems or opportunities that surface. *There are no exceptions if one wants to be a member of the clan* because shared leadership is based on talent, skills, and experience and not on the specific position one holds in an organization. That is precisely one of the main reasons for the vigorous selection process discussed earlier.

It takes considerable energy, self-initiative, mental toughness and never ending persistence (besides one's abilities) to work in an overt self-organizing environment. There is no place to hide. You are either in or out of the game since there is no place to sit on the sidelines and watch the action. Although the rewards can be tremendous, not everyone is prepared to devote so much time and energy to a venture. That's especially true of people who have become accustomed to relatively unchallenging and uninspiring 8 to 5 occupations.

Consensus decision-making, like shared leadership, is a fluid process that helps to provide an organization dynamic alignment. Organizational alignment has nothing in common with maintaining control. It's all about sustaining dynamic order as discussed in Chapters Four and Seven. In a controlled-access structure official control systems are a necessity by design since only designated people have the authority to make alignment corrections or change course altogether. Everyone else seldom has the will or nerve to offer proposals openly (even official suggestion programs rarely ever produce any worthwhile results) not to mention the courage to offer assistance to steer the ship.

In a self-organizing system the opposite is true. Everybody feels personally responsible and accountable for the success or failure of the entire operation. They also have learned that major accomplishments are only possible through voluntary, tightly-coupled interdependent actions. Thus, in order to maintain or regain positive dynamic order, consensus decision-making and open dialogue are the most viable options in conjunction with shared or situational leadership. How else is it really possible to keep *all members* aligned in such an open arrangement? Everyone must be involved, or at least knowledgeable, about all the activities of the clan.

Finally, it is also critical that all members of a shared-access framework be familiar and at ease with systems thinking. Perceiving wholes instead of individual parts or components is not something most of us have learned in school or at work. That is, being able to visualize how all the pieces (processes, teams, departments, branches, divisions, etc.) of an organization must work together in order to produce a product or provide a service has rarely, if ever, been an essential element of a job description in a controlled-access system. That is left to the bosses or planning departments. Is it a wonder then that most people in hierarchical establishments don't know and, as a consequence, don't care how their part of the operation affects others, not to mention customers?

As mentioned previously, a shared-access system is a parallel operating system where everything works together simultaneously by means of circular causality. Hence, every constituent (individuals and teams) must know exactly what everyone else is doing in order to make sure that their activities support, and not hinder, what is taking place in the rest of the establishment. Overt self-organization demands that all elements of a system be capable of functioning both autonomously and interdependently at the same time assuring that local and large-scale activities are synchronized. Without systems thinking, that is impossible to accomplish effectively.

3.   THE BALANCED EXPRESSION OF OUR INNATE DRIVES

It is now time to recap what we have learned about the model representing the four principles of open self-organization and to suggest how an organization can begin to incorporate the system into its specific framework. Reluctantly (because of my previous note of caution), I will also present an example of a company that has functioned successfully in a shared-access mode for over 40 years at the end of the chapter.

Three significant aspects about social institutions need to be kept in mind as we take a summary look at Figure 5-1 and progress through the rest of the book. First, informal groups and networks emerge *voluntarily* in every organization in order to satisfy human genetic predispositions, which have evolved to help us better cope with our immediate environments. Put another way, we naturally self-organize by means of circular causality in the pursuit of life's common purpose (living long enough to perpetuate the species) as described in Chapter Three. The development of these informal associations can't be controlled, avoided or circumvented.

Second, humans function best when both their self-centered and other-centered innate drives have an opportunity to be expressed in a balanced manner. The balanced activation of these genetic predispositions can only take place in a social context where trust, interdependence, and reciprocity are practiced unreservedly. *Voluntary* collaboration is the foundation of all informal networks. That is precisely why these self-organizing groups *emerge* and can't be formally controlled or managed.

Lastly, mandated activities, interactions, and behaviors drive informal groups underground. Unseen, these clusters of people may support or oppose, supplement or sabotage or have no impact at all on the formal organization. Although the informal networks can't be controlled, I am rather surprised why so far no serious attempt has been made to support them openly. As a result, the power of the invisible networks (where most of the work in organizations is accomplished in the first place) is hardly ever fully tapped. We can now begin to grasp why so many institutes are short of social capital. The framework depicted by Figure 5-1 is intended to alleviate that situation for enterprises interested in leveraging their invisible assets.

While we can easily see the four distinct principles and what they delineate as portrayed by the model, it's also apparent that their actions and interactions are tightly coupled. Any one of the individual principles can't *fully* function without the support of the other three. For instance, individual autonomy, even when well meshed with shared identity, still can't produce the intended results without the support of challenging aspirations and dynamic alignment. Hence, every principle needs to be "up and running" before the system can supply the necessary dynamics required to suitably foster the activities of informal networks openly.

It's also apparent that the system does not rely on any prescribed formal structure or control mechanisms. Instead, there are ample real time feedback and feedforward loops (discussed in Chapter Seven) represented by the overlapping circles. The sharing of information is further enhanced by frequent face-to-face and virtual interactions between clan members. In essence, the clan stays on track by means of shared leadership and consensus decision-making. Thus, a self-organizing system is reliant on voluntary collaboration and form without an officially imposed structure. It's akin to an amoeba altering its shape as environmental conditions change and new opportunities appear.

The importance of the four interrelated principles, not only for a self-organizing group but for any well functioning innovative enterprise, has been a "no-brainer" for me for years. Sadly, that view, even though verbally espoused by many top executives (largely in reference to shared identity or culture), is seldom actually put into practice in most companies. For those who still have some doubt regarding the true significance of the principles to an organization, let me briefly summarize several key conclusions reached by a recent study. Granted, many of the specific details and the integrated framework that I've presented weren't part of the inquiry but, clearly, the overall results support my model.

Essentially, the researchers sought to identify distinctive elements of highly innovation-supportive cultures in real-life product innovation settings. Below are some of their key findings:

Guiding values, beliefs, and assumptions of participants in innovation-supportive cultures:

- Taking initiative and exhibiting creativity and risk-taking are important and expected.
- All participants are capable of being trusted in a co-creative endeavor and are important, equal stakeholders.
- All participants (including leading customers, key suppliers, and members of other functional groups) are *insiders* and should be involved early in the product-development process.
- Organizational change is energizing and refreshing. Change should be embraced rather than resisted.

Behaviors:

- Participants voice the clear sense of control that they feel about their involvement in the new-product development process.
- Participants exhibit high levels of co-creative, collaborative behaviors.
- Participants show willingness to make themselves vulnerable to feedback from others.

Related new-product outcomes:

New products from new technologies are developed within time and cost budgets and achieve market success.[8]

These conclusions clearly indicate the types of organizational contexts that need to be developed for knowledge professionals and for any enterprise wishing to succeed in the Knowledge Age. Figure 5-1 and other integrated models described in the chapters that follow provide a practical road map as to bring that about.

4. GETTING STARTED

The logical question now is, "How do you begin to actually incorporate the framework of the model into an existing organization or a start-up?" As one might presume, the system is relatively straight forward, having existed for at least 200,000 years, but its implementation takes a great deal of effort and dogged persistence. That is especially the case for existing institutions.

It's not easy because 99 percent of us have never had the opportunity to work or live in a shared-access environment other than among our families and friendship groups (that may not always be true either). Being constantly surrounded by and working in controlled-access organizations has given us the perception that hierarchical structures are natural and unavoidable. Of course, that really isn't true and we do have a choice.

People in an organization who decide to change from a controlled-access to a shared-access operation must first be thoroughly convinced that such a change is the best option for the future so that they will not vacillate about the resolution. The attempt to switch from conventional management to unmanagement should not be taken lightly since here we are not dealing with a *new* management method, procedure, or process such as total quality management or self-managing teams which, essentially, leave the hierarchy (tall or flat) intact.

Adopting the principles of unmanagement demands completely rethinking the way an organization should function. Rethinking means discarding conventional approaches altogether instead of trying to refine them. That is why I added the "un" to management.

In a shared-access system there is no place for "employees", but plenty of room for partners who are ready to roll up their sleeves and voluntarily pursue challenging and aspiring goals. There also is no place for supervisors or managers and the power that goes with those positions because there is "no bossing." There are, however, boundless opportunities for talented people to take the lead, with the support of their colleagues, as new vistas constantly appear over the horizon.

Once the choice is made to proceed *there are no lock-step procedures to follow*. Each organization, through experimentation and using the four principles as a guide, must fashion its own unique organizational context that will help its informal groups and networks take center stage. To help get the process started there are some general guidelines that people can follow.

First, in an existing organization the CEO and his or her executive staff must make that final assessment. We are all well aware of the fact that without the full commitment (versus permission) of top management, nothing earthshaking will ever transpire. At the same time "public assurances" need to be made by top executives that position power, at all levels of the enterprise, will be phased out by the end of the conversion period and that the administrators will find other ways to put their talents to use in the enterprise. A complete switchover to the new model must be made. An organization can't just adopt parts of the new framework. In a start-up the decision to incorporate all aspects of a self-organizing system is simply made when a company is initially formed.

Second, it's wise to engage someone who is thoroughly familiar with the shared-access principles to reassure that all concerned are interpreting the workings of the model correctly. Yet, from the outset, it should be clear that the expert is only responsible for initial education and coaching concerning the details of the model. He/she provides the guidelines as to *what* should be accomplished but, categorically, not *how* the process is carried out. The "how" segment of the conversion or initial incorporation in start-ups must be left to the members of an organization themselves.

The end product is an overt and not a covert self-organizing system. Therefore, clan members, who are literally building a new social context for themselves, must do all the planning and implementing of those plans. Without voluntary collaboration by all members of the firm, open self-organization isn't possible.

A consultant or coach can be a sounding board and provide valuable advice, but he or she will never be a permanent member of the enterprise. As an outsider, the advisor can seldom become an intimate member of the self-organizing system that he or she is helping to get off the ground. Sooner or later they walk away when their work is done. Thus, in a shared-access system everyone "makes his or her own bed." Maid services are only provided in controlled-access firms and they are costly.

Third, after all members have a thorough understanding of the self-organizing principles, which should not take more than two to three days, they should be encouraged to form small groups around the company's core competencies. Remember, core competencies are not the products or services of an enterprise. Rather, they are the talents of an organization much similar to those of an individual. These competencies (unique technologies, special processes, extraordinary networking abilities, and so on) provide the basis for products and services but are much broader and flexible, to be relied on as conditions change.

Fourth, once these small groups (not more than about 6 to 12 people in a group) are formed, they then begin the arduous task of conceptualizing and planning as to how work should be conducted around and between specific core competencies and outside constituents (major suppliers, clients, etc.). After these initial plans are completed, all the groups then come together to share what they have developed in order to learn from each other and to make sure their plans are not in conflict. This process is repeated until all concerned are satisfied with the plans. It is quite apparent that shared leadership, consensus decision-making, and systems thinking need to be practiced right from the outset.

Finally, it's at this juncture when the implementation of the agreed upon procedures begin. Throughout the execution phase the same groups continue to meet for the same reasons as during the planning stage. Clearly, the planning and execution phases should be self-organizing processes governed by circular causality. People learn through trial and error as they continue to change the organization. There actually is no end to this course of action since there is no perfect system at the end of the rainbow. As we are well aware, conditions change and so do people's goals and aspirations.

Undoubtedly, there is much more that takes place while the participants are rethinking what the best options are and how to apply them. Recall that change is also physiological, not just psychological. Therefore, it takes time for people to build up and engage unused neurological pathways so that they can "thicken" by regular use. Also, as free wheeling teams begin to emerge within the newly established framework they will most likely need some team development training and facilitation. Such training, however, should not be conducted across-the-board but, instead, it should be made available to teams as they request it. It is also recommended that an outside expert visit the organization periodically in order to make independent assessments and to provide feedback concerning the progress of the change initiative.

5. AN EXAMPLE—W. L. GORE & ASSOCIATES

To me W.L. Gore & Associates is one of the best examples of an enterprise that uses overt self-organization to the limit. Gore is a privately held firm headquartered in Newark, Delaware with over 6,000 associates working in 45 locations around the world, with annual sales of over one billion dollars. Founded by Wilbert (Bill) Gore and his wife Genevieve (Vieve) in their basement in 1958, the company has operated in a shared-access mode from the beginning. Hence, it's not hard to imagine why they have repeatedly been named among the "100 Best Companies to Work for in America".

While they are best known for GORE-TEX® fabrics, all their products and teams are distinguished in their markets. Gore's technologies and fluoropolymer expertise are unsurpassed. For example, they have advanced the science of regenerating tissue destroyed by disease or traumatic injuries, developed next-generation materials for printed circuit boards and fiber optics, and pioneered new methods to detect and control environmental pollution

Bill and Vieve organized the firm around "real teams" and insisted that associates make their own commitments and stick to them. Thus, from day one they had no use for managers. The emphasis was put on shared leadership grounded in talent, expertise, and drive rather than on position power. This open self-organizing work context gives everyone involved the opportunity to find where they can best put their abilities to work for both their own and the company's benefit since everyone has a stake in the action. Sticky administrative situations are deliberately avoided.

Further, the organization has a "lattice communications network" which permits and encourages each associate to contact any affiliate of the 45 plants around the world when a problem needs to be quickly resolved or an opportunity requires immediate attention. Also of interest is the fact that none of the plants, by design, have more than 200 members. Bill and Vieve knew more than 40 years ago that clans could outperform larger entities.

Gore's philosophy is very simple but powerful. They have one fundamental objective and four guiding principles. Their objective is, "To make money and have fun." The founders believed that the process of accomplishing organizational goals should be both fun and meaningful. The four principles are equally clear-cut. The first is *fairness,* meaning that all associates should be fair with each other, with customers, with suppliers, and with the communities where they work. Second is *freedom.* Every person at Gore is encouraged to innovate and experiment with new ideas. Bill and Vieve believed that everyone should help their fellow associates to grow in knowledge, responsibilities, and range of activities. Leadership is earned through talented performance without the use of "bossing" or position power.

Commitment is the third principle. It contends that each associate must make their own commitments and keep them. Hence, no one can impose a commitment on another. The final principle is labeled *waterline.* What it means is that an organization is like a ship at sea. Boring holes above the waterline is not dangerous but doing so below the waterline has serious consequences. Thus, every associate, before taking any action that may cause serious harm to the reputation, success, or survival of the firm, must first consult with appropriate colleagues who will share in the responsibility of the action.[9]

It is quite clear that W.L. Gore and Associates has an extended track record in knowing how to tap into the power of the invisible mother lode of social systems. It is high time that other organizations learn to do the same *in their own way.*

Chapter 6

CULTIVATING "NO BOSSING" LEADERSHIP

Leadership is an important "dynamic" of any social group. For this reason it's also central to a well functioning shared-access system. Leadership is a dynamic phenomenon since it *emerges* under all sorts of settings and, therefore, is unavoidable just like the appearance of informal networks.

Countless people, however, fail to differentiate between true leadership and hierarchical position power. The distinctions are quite significant. Designated roles in top-down institutions attain their status through *resource holding power* as did our distant ancestors more than 300 million years ago (see Chapter Three). Conversely, emergent leaders earn their status by means of *social attention holding potential* which is more in step with our less distant relatives and modern humans.

Position power is based on coercion (no matter how benevolent) and demands *compliance* from subordinates in following directives. Natural leadership is situational based on talent, expertise, and the demands of a particular state of affairs and is reliant on the *commitment* of followers to a common goal. The former is an indispensable part of a controlled-access venture. The latter fits the self-organizing dynamics of a shared-access system. As one can see, the differences are rather noteworthy. The spotlight in this chapter is on these dissimilarities both from a historical and practical perspective.

1.   LEADERSHIP DEFINED

"Genuine" leaders are able to perceive certain situations from a different or clearer and less ambiguous perspective. They have a strong drive and are willing to assume personal responsibility to complete a task, solve a pressing problem or take advantage of an opportunity. Accordingly, leaders are individuals who can take a confusing or complex state of affairs and frame it in such a way that others are capable of comprehending it and *willing* to take appropriate action. Another important aspect of leadership is trust. Thus, great leaders are well aware of the value of trust based on strong personal bonds versus trust founded on expertise and structural relationships (primarily hierarchical associations in controlled-access systems). Genuine leaders also have high levels of synthesized intelligence, creativity, and wisdom.[1]

Anyone is capable of being a leader. Depending on their talents, skills, and experiences certain people are able to assume leadership roles more often than others, but each one of us has the capacity to lead. It may be a small event or something monumental. When and what a person takes charge of depends on their background, chance, the group involved, and the situation. Thus, whether we are a world-renowned expert or a relatively anonymous being, we can and should "take the wheel" when the right occasion presents itself while others, at least momentarily, look to us for guidance.

There are as many definitions of leadership as there have been writers on the subject. What that suggests to me is that leadership doesn't have an exact form that can be codified and followed. Therefore, like an individual's unique personality, it is a tacit distinctive part of every person that can't be completely emulated by others. So, if someone attempts to sell you a ten step leadership formula guaranteeing success in the future (and many will repeatedly try), keep a firm hand on your purse or wallet.

Let me offer you my definition of leadership at the outset giving you a better opportunity to determine if my description remains valid by the end of the chapter. From my perspective the "no bossing" or emergent leadership process is defined as follows:

> **Helping others to initiate or participate in worthwhile activities that they are either not aware of or are hesitant to take action on their own, which would benefit everyone involved.**

2.   LEADERSHIP AND SELF-ORGANIZING SYSTEMS

The most fundamental question that we need to answer first is, "Can self-organizing systems have a permanently (relatively speaking) assigned leader?" In search of the most rational answer to that question we need to again revisit our ancient past. Put another way, if informal bands and networks were the most successful social adaptations of our kind for 99 percent of our existence on the planet, then how did leadership fit into this framework?

As stipulated previously, the latest scientific evidence suggests our hunter-gatherer ancestors practiced shared or situational leadership. Why? They certainly could have used the "winner takes all" option or the "king of the mountain" (hierarchical) alternative, since we still possess those genetic predispositions. We know that it was not a random choice since life's common purpose (surviving long enough to perpetuate the species) and the evolutionary process hardly would have permitted that to happen.

Three modes of competition. Recollect more than 300 million years ago our ancient forbearers competed for food, territory and mates individually as many vertebrates continue to do today (see Figure 3-2). About 100 million years later as group living began to be more advantageous and territory began to be shared, competition for higher rank, rather than terrain, became the principle form for maintaining relationships within social groups. Thus, competition by domination, instead of winner takes all, became the principal means for attaining individual resource holding power and for maintaining group stability. Its downside was the constant social tension that existed in these communities.

Starting roughly ten million years ago, and at an accelerated pace in the past two million years among primates and hominids (our closest cousins), a new form of competition began to emerge. Instead of attempting to intimidate and dominate rivals, individuals now began to attract them to participate in voluntary and mutually beneficial activities. In the process they increased their status and resource attention holding potential. There was an added benefit. The attraction mode of interaction, because it was based on voluntary cooperation, eliminated the constant psychological tension present in hierarchical groups.

What was the underlying reason for the changes in the survival modes of living systems over time? You may already have intuitively answered that question. I suggest that the explanation for the transformation of the survival modes was (and still is) caused by the continuous search by biological forms for more efficient ways of resource acquisition and distribution. After all, that is the basis for evolution.

From single cells to complex configurations, all organisms are self-organizing structures. That means that each biological entity is a self-contained system able to fend for itself at least for a limited time. Therefore, more than 300 million years ago the most efficient way for survival was to compete individually for food, territory, and mates. Later, as the brainpower of certain life forms increased, it became more productive for those species to live in small hierarchical groups.

Each member of those bands, however, still remained a complete self-organizing entity innately looking out for his or her own welfare. As a result, lower ranking individuals devoted considerable time and energy to self-centered covert activities to satisfy their own particular needs. These activities were conducted secretly, out of sight of high-ranking members, in order to avoid punishment. Clearly, the group's overall efficiency suffered in the process since much of everyone's attention was not primarily focused on common goals.

As even more complex organisms evolved, the less efficient hierarchical social groups began to be replaced by overtly self-organized clans founded on competition by attraction rather than domination. Thus, eliminating the need of lower ranking members to waste time and effort in clandestine activities increased the total group effectiveness. One can now begin to make the connection between my definition of true leadership and competition by attraction versus position power (rank and intimidation). I will come back to this point momentarily.

Position power and self-organizing systems. So, is there a place for permanent leadership or power based on rank in overt self-organizing systems? As mentioned earlier, biological entities are self-organizing systems down to their individual DNA molecules. Hence, there are certain biological constraints imposed on us but there is no master plan or are there guidelines specifying exactly how we must respond to environmental conditions. The same is true of a social institution. People will self-organize no matter what situation they find themselves in. It's an unpreventable and unstoppable natural process. It is a course of action, based on people's perceptions relative to their individual survival options, that can't be *controlled* by anything or anybody.

Self-organization is governed by circular causality, individual status (as opposed to rank), and attraction (not intimidation). Rank is simply another barrier to be overcome. If necessary, like an amoeba, a self-organizing system will eventually go through, over, around or under the barrier or change direction altogether. Hence, how a person or informal group goes about pursuing its goals is not exactly predictable. It's all about establishing and maintaining dynamic order (positive or negative) in the pursuit of our most favorable survival opportunities.

What we can foresee, however, is that any entity that hasn't become part of the naturally formed self-organizing framework through the process of circular causality, or worse is imposed on it, can't be totally accepted by the system. Therefore, they are either tolerated to one degree or another or are totally rejected, but never seen as a full-fledged member of the group. Of course, we all know that rejections can come in many varieties from violent confrontations to pleasant smiles and cordial handshakes without any intent of cooperation. The process is identical to how our bodies tolerate or battle foreign objects and diseases.

I think we can now safely conclude that there is no place for leadership based on rank in a genuine self-organizing system. Imposed leadership is equivalent to a "foreign object" and the most that can be expected from an informal group is some tolerance of it. Thus, in a shared-access environment there can't be any "rank barriers" to go through when it comes to decision-making, allocating resources, dealing with suppliers or interacting with customers and other external networks.

Another look at my definition of leadership shows that the process needs to be thoroughly grounded in noninterference mutualism or voluntary cooperation that is beneficial for all concerned. Simply put, rank pushes self-organization underground reducing the overall effectiveness of a group. "Alphas" are an effective component of wolf packs but not for human communities dependent on high levels of social capital for leveraging their knowledge to the fullest extent possible.

3.   REEMERGENCE OF RANK AND CONTROLLED-ACCESS SYSTEMS

So, if hierarchical leadership is less efficient than shared or situational leadership, then what are the reasons for its gradual reemergence in roughly the past 15 thousand years? As I discussed in Chapter Three, both nature and our own kind have contributed to the collapse of the most successful and longitudinal human social adaptation to date, the hunter-gatherer way of life. It happened very slowly and, ironically, the general structure that began to gradually dominate most forms of social relationships was the survival mode that our ancient ancestors began to abandon ten million years earlier.

With the flooding of the coastal lowlands and rapidly spreading forests the hunter-gatherers were constrained to smaller and smaller geographic areas and, therefore, became less mobile. As travel became more restricted and demanding, populations also increased in these enclaves. This, in turn, led to the founding of agriculture and the domestication of animals. Thus, the stage was set for the proliferation of increasingly larger and more complex organizational frameworks and the re-emergence of leadership based on position power.

As individual tribes grew to more than 150 members, three principal factors contributed to the reemergence of hierarchies. One was the ability to produce and store excess food and other resources brought about by the introduction of farming. The second was the permanent settlement of productive land areas and with it the introduction of property ownership. The third factor was the increased size of the population centers that made it impossible for people to be well acquainted with everyone, to practice consensus decision-making, or to coordinate important community wide activities.[2]

We must remind ourselves that evolution doesn't create completely original life forms unless, of course, we go back to the beginning of life on earth almost four billion years ago. Even that may not be the case if organic matter was deposited by the frequent impact of stellar bodies at the early stages of our planet's development. What that means is that the evolutionary process allows organisms to adapt to existing environmental conditions and not to anticipated circumstances. Therefore, when situations change (gradually or by a large meteorite impact) living systems must either acclimate or vanish. Those that are able to adapt, however, do not completely discard their evolutionary past but rather carry it forward with them. That is why, for instance, we still have much in common genetically even with the lowly sea slug.

What I am getting at is that all of the three survival modes that have evolved over millions of years are all still part of our genetic make-up. There is ample evidence in the daily news and our lives in general that evolution over the eons has not turned us into "saints" by any stretch of the imagination. Consequently, as the social context of human communities changed quite significantly shortly after the last Ice Age, so did the use of our fundamental survival strategies.

Gradually, as the size of permanent settlements grew, altruism and reciprocity no longer were the best options for survival other than within small informal groups of kin and close friends. Of course, mutually beneficial exchanges could be made in the market places but that did not equate to the egalitarianism practiced by the immediate consumption hunter-gathers for several hundred thousand years before the age of agriculture.

Changes in the social fabric were slow and subtle. Resources produced by agriculture were not immediately consumed and, therefore, had to be stored. Also, the assets one accumulated could now be kept hidden from the rest of the community since most people owned their own land and dwellings and, therefore, no longer needed to be prepared to carry everything they owned on their backs.

Thus, the shame and guilt (part of our innate drives) of not sharing resources with clan members was easier to overcome, especially during the initial stages of agriculture. A modern day example of this clandestine activity is the diligence with which we keep our bank accounts and incomes a secret, often even from family members.

Finally, in settlements of more than 150 members close mutually caring contact with everyone was no longer possible resulting in most folks becoming relative "strangers" to one another. As a result, reciprocity and consensus decision-making on a community wide basis faded away and were gradually replaced by all encompassing formal social structures headed by the more affluent members of the society.

In addition, specialization of work and division of labor became increasingly necessary in supporting these larger centralized populations. As a consequence, most people no longer owned their own means of production and became dependent on more prosperous individuals and institutions. Predictably, before long position power and class differences became prominent and widespread.

Clearly, without high levels of trust and mutualism, a shared-access approach was no longer the best option for survival. Essentially, the new social context did not penalize people for being selfish by reducing their social status. In fact, it encouraged hoarding and the use of our most basic competitive mode. "Winner takes all" and "king of the mountain" again became the best options for survival. There was little need for high levels of social capital.

As class differences emerged it became more and more acceptable to exhibit one's rank and status through all sorts of grandiose monuments, temples and opulence in general. Ironically, to further boost their status and to lessen their feelings of guilt, some prosperous individuals also began to partake in charitable activities. As one can readily see, not much has changed to the present day. I don't need to take this further because the rest is well documented by historians. However, it should be noted that we are yet to develop an *enduring* large complex "civilization". Why?

I believe our inability to build large lasting social frameworks is relatively straightforward. Most people have yet to grasp who we are as human beings and what it takes to satisfy our innate drives in a balanced manner. Therefore, we have failed to seriously consider leveraging the tremendous wealth, knowledge, and power of our informal self-organizing systems. With our continuing worship of the hierarchy, the invisible "mother lode" remains mostly hidden in the underground labyrinths.

Simply put, societies based on greed and position power do not have lasting appeal for the majority of its citizens. Paradoxically, developing social systems where our innate drives have an opportunity to be expressed in an evenhanded fashion has little relevancy with "equality" (genetically we are all unequal) but a great deal to do with "equity." I will elaborate on the difference in Chapter Seven.

If the hierarchy isn't the most efficient means of resource management and distribution, then why is it continuing to be used? The answer to that question is straightforward—excess accumulation of resources. Starting about 12,000 years ago we began to cultivate plants and domesticate animals, accruing excess resources in the process. Later, with the proliferation of commerce, even more wealth was amassed. What this means is that large more technologically advanced societies have gathered sufficient resources that act as a buffer against environmental uncertainties.

This benefit, however, has come at a considerable human cost. As they say, "There is no such thing as a free lunch." The price tag includes workplace inefficiencies, minimal leisure time, resource distribution inequities, dependence, alienation, negative politics, family stress, crime and violence, not to mention rampant greed. It's all recorded in our local and national newspapers daily.

The negative affects of controlled-access institutions should not come as a big surprise to us. Having developed, and continuing to exist in, organizational contexts where our most basic self-centered drives are constantly being bombarded by intimidating stimuli, what else should we expect? What is most disheartening to me is that given a choice most people would prefer to work and live in shared-access environments. Hence, there is no doubt that our altruistic genetic tendencies are alive and well. Will we, however, have the courage to change our social institutions to support their expression in the years to come? History will tell.

4.   FOUNDATIONS OF CURRENT LEADERSHIP THEORIES

At the beginning of the chapter I mentioned that there are as many "recognized" theories of leadership as there have been writers on the subject (for proof do a quick search on the Internet). There are thousands of more "unofficial" thoughts regarding the topic that have yet to see daylight since most everyone seems to have their own opinions on the matter. The ideas I will present are wholly founded on human nature and the principles of self-organizing systems. Accordingly, I will first identify the focus of current popular leadership theories and then present my own general model of no bossing, or emergent leadership, based on commitment not compliance.

A brief historical overview. Starting with the Sumerians about 5,000 B.C. and continuing with the Egyptians, Chinese, Greeks, Romans, Venetians and others, much has been written about the administration of large complex organizations. During the course of the Industrial Revolution, ideas about management were further advanced by the   writings of prominent economists and industry leaders such as Adam Smith and James Watt.[3]

Finally, at the beginning of the last century three world-renowned figures set the stage for management thinking and research for the remainder of the industrial era. They were Max Weber, author of *The Theory of Social and Economic Organization;* Henri Fayol, who wrote *General and Industrial Management;* and Frederick M. Taylor, who became the leading management guru of his time with the publication of *The Principles of Scientific Management.*[4] In my opinion, what has evolved in the annals of management thinking since these classic works appeared almost 100 years ago has basically been more rigorous refinement of the fundamental ideas presented by the three legendary authors.

Not unexpectedly, the topic of leadership has followed the same path since the advent of written history. Thus, with rare exception, almost all of the research and literature on the subject has revolved around the "anointed" man or woman charged with the affairs of private or public institutions. That is, the focus, especially since recorded history, has been nearly exclusively on how best to attain and apply position power.

From a progression perspective, competition by intimidation and domination, rather than by competition by attraction and voluntary cooperation, has monopolized our accepted wisdom concerning leadership. Until very recently, rethinking simply hasn't even been in the cards. This is a good example of how research in any field seldom strays far from the conventional mindset. No wonder the invisible underpinnings of our organizations have been, and remain, largely untapped.

Classical theories of leadership. Before presenting my own ideas regarding leadership I need to provide more details with reference to existing theories so that I can better contrast current thinking with my own perspectives on the subject.[5] Probably the most appropriate way to begin that process is to mention some of the so-called "classical" theories of leadership. They are classical because they have been around for quite some time, are part of the management curriculum of most universities, and are still widely used in our organizations. What they all have in common is that their focus is exclusively on *assigned leadership* or legitimized position power.

The coverage of classical leadership theories typically begins with the trait approach (originally designated as the "great man theory"). As one can speculate, considerable time and effort was wasted on attempts to define specific mental, psychological, and physical qualities associated with leadership success so that such a framework could be used to select "great men" for top positions.

Eventually, it was determined that leaders come in all sorts of shapes and sizes and that intelligence, self-confidence, courage and so on also appear in a variety of forms. Obviously, whoever was in charge needed to have some aptitude but, other than that, the rest remained a mystery. Today important traits are considered to be such qualities as decisiveness, knowledge, adaptability, integrity, sociability, and diplomacy. That, in my humble opinion, really does not add much to the usefulness of trait theories.

Next, we have the behavioral theories of leadership. What they advocate is that successful administrators should not focus exclusively on either people or production. They must learn how to properly balance their attention on both factors. If that is not sufficient in order to become a great captain of industry we can turn to the Contingency Theory. The contingency approach suggests that a good leader can determine what style of management to exercise by first determining what type of situation they are faced with. Once that has been accomplished they then select one of three styles of leadership—task oriented, relations oriented, or a combination of both—to keep the troops in line.

Then, of course, there is the Path-Goal-Theory. According to this theory the leader's primary task is to define an employee's job and the best path to reach his or her work goals. The most appropriate way to do that is for the boss to match the right leadership style with the characteristics of the followers. Finally, if all else fails, one can always turn to the Life-Cycle Model of Situational Leadership. In applying this model a bright manager can select one of four styles of leadership depending on the "readiness" of his or her followers. The styles include telling, selling, participating, and delegating.

I do not think I need to go any further with the classical leadership theories. I believe it is quite clear that, even under the most stringent controlled-access conditions, these guidelines can, at best, only be of limited aid to aspiring administrators.

Current theories of leadership. Six "modern" theories of leadership have gotten considerable attention during the past fifteen years. Two of the six theories have emerged just recently. One is Super Leadership, which advocates encouraging followers to becoming self-leaders. There is nothing wrong with this concept except that the super leader does not give up his or her "throne" in the organization once everyone else has passed the self-leadership test. I suppose the super star has to keep his or her rank permanently (relatively speaking) in order to assure self-leadership is fully adhered to.

Transformational Leadership is another theory that is still quite popular. This model suggests that excellent top executives accomplish three things to keep their posts. First, they must recognize the need for organizational revitalization. Next, a new vision needs to be created. Finally, the transformation has to be institutionalized. Of course, this process is repeated again as conditions change. How can something be truly institutionalized without also seriously engaging the informal part of an organization?

The last two theories remind me of Mikhail Gorbachev's attempt to transform communism into a gentler and kinder version in the former Soviet Union. As we all know his endeavor failed because he had no intention of changing the fundamental framework of the communist system. The same is true with efforts to reform and streamline hierarchies. Tall, flat or placid, a controlled-access system is founded on rank, domination and control. Also, as is the case with communism, the deficiencies of hierarchies are unavoidable.[6]

The other four theories in vogue today are Stewardship, Servant Leadership, Primal Leadership, and Level 5 Leadership. The last two are the most recent additions.[7] The first recommends that people in top positions guide followers into becoming responsible team players. The second proposes that leaders be individuals who are willing to devote their efforts to serving others in accomplishing common goals. The third suggests that positive emotions are contagious. The fourth stipulates that the most effective leaders who help build enduring organizational greatness are not the high-profile types who make headlines. Instead they "are a paradoxical blend of personal humility and professional will." How can anyone disagree with these leadership philosophies?

Such leaders are absolutely vital in converting hierarchies into shared-access systems of the future. However, what must also be plainly understood is that once the transformation is completed these leaders, like everyone else, must relinquish their status based on rank (position power) and maintain their status in the group by adhering to the principles of emergent or "no bossing" leadership (discussed shortly).

The key dynamics of current leadership theories. Let me summarize four key dynamics that need to be kept in mind with reference to the current theories of leadership. First, we need to admit that controlled-access systems managed with rank hierarchies are not the most efficient or human friendly entities. The fact is that many social institutions can be changed to eliminate those deficiencies *if* we so desire. Second, as mentioned previously, flat or tall, run by a tyrant or a super leader, a hierarchy is a hierarchy no matter how its seats of power are masked.

Third, no one born to date has the intelligence, talent, or energy to be the perfect leader for all occasions. You can take the smartest and most charismatic person in the world and strap a super computer under each arm and they still couldn't that ideal leader. Yet, strangely enough, we thoughtlessly expect that feat to be accomplished daily by the elected and appointed leaders of our public and private institutions.

Certain leaders can be, and are in most instances, assisted by expert staffs in their decision-making processes. However, who makes the final decision and how much does that individual heed the advice given to him or her? In many instances aren't we literally setting people up for failure? Why don't we spread the organizational responsibility and accountability more evenly around instead of expediently looking for a scapegoat when things go wrong? If we are serious about developing much more effective enterprises we need to be prepared to answer these questions honestly.

Finally, there is a very dark and seldom talked about side to the use of position power. Doling out rewards (bonuses, salaries, choice assignments, office space, etc.) can be exercised very coercively, sometimes even by well meaning people. Much more demoralizing is the frequent application of position power or "legitimate" power. There really is no position or legitimate power. The only way a person is able to have more power over others is for followers to either willingly, or by some form of intimidation give up some of theirs.

In any case, the more frequently people use position power the more comfortable they become with its application. Eventually these individuals begin to devalue subordinates by attributing their performance to the frequent employment of their power rather than the abilities and motivation of the underlings. Repeated users of position authority also like to maintain psychological distance from their employees and believe that it is acceptable to use manipulative skills for leadership effectiveness.[8]

That shouldn't come as a surprise. We know that the repeated use of our most basic genetic inclinations (such as rank and domination) strengthen the neural pathways associated with those drives. Of course, the same is true when it comes to the recurring expression of our other-centered genetic tendencies. As a result, given the appropriate surroundings, humans can be both the most brutal and the most compassionate organisms on our planet.

This is another vivid example of why it is imperative that our social institutions be designed in such a way that people's innate drives can be expressed in a balanced manner. It also shows that current theories of leadership fail to seriously address the gap that exists between structural hypotheses and motivational schemes. Such theories can't possibly result in long-range organizational success (as validated by past and present events) since they ignore the power of human nature.

5.   ELEMENTS OF "NO BOSSING" LEADERSHIP

Emergent leadership is a requisite and inevitable component of human social groups. It is a natural dynamic part of the self-organizing process. Position power, however, is not. It is an imposition and is dealt with accordingly (politely or otherwise) by the people associated with it. Consequently, from my standpoint, designated leaders can rarely be considered to be "genuine" leaders. Only emergent leaders have earned the respect of the people who *willingly* follow them. That esteem also constantly needs to be reacquired as conditions change because, unlike position power, shared leadership is situational and fluid.

No bossing leadership is characterized by emergent behavior of individuals attempting to facilitate the integration of people's personal goals and aspirations with the vision of a given social entity as a whole. It's a process of continuous change where different individuals (depending on their talents, skills, and expertise) are looked to for guidance and advice as a group is faced with different internal and external circumstances. It's founded on voluntary actions intended for mutual benefits and involves no intimidation or bossing. In essence, no one gives up his or her autonomy or power in the process.

Possible concerns. Clearly, the two paragraphs above leave me open for all sorts of questions and arguments. Let me try to put three of the most apparent queries to rest before we take a closer look at my model. First, does my argument apply to elected office holders? Only if these individuals are chosen by an actual democratic process without all sorts of back office deals and other unethical practices and the constituents are limited to no more than 150 people. Also, unless the people who work with an elected official are volunteers or partners/equals, one is again faced with the dynamics of a hierarchy.

Second, is it possible for appointed people to gain the genuine respect of their followers or will they always be perceived as outsiders? It is possible but it rarely happens since there are considerable built-in hurdles to overcome. Under the right circumstances an individual could find himself or herself in a situation where they clearly have the precise talents, skills, background, and social relationships (the right stuff) to be looked to as the natural leader for the circumstances. Secretary of State, Colin Powell, is an example of such an individual in the midst of the current Mideast and worldwide terrorism crisis. Of course, he also believes that, "Leadership is not rank, privilege, titles, or money. It's responsibility."[9]

Also, people who work for an appointed leader rarely can, or want to, have a very close relationship with that person. The same is true from the leader's perspective. This doesn't mean that chosen or selected heads of organizations can't be fully respected and admired. They most definitely can be. From a self-organizing standpoint, however, these people are restricted to their own informal circles of friends, relatives, and its associated group dynamics, which seldom include any of the individuals working for them.

Finally, is there a need for appointed leadership? Absolutely. Organizations composed of more than 150 members are usually unable to properly coordinate their activities without some types of top down systems unless some very drastic changes are made in their structures. Moreover, certain critical societal components such as the police, firefighters, and military must respond instantaneously to unanticipated events. There simply is no time in those organizations for lengthy deliberations when they are operating under emergency conditions.

As a volunteer who served twenty years in the United States Air Force, I have great respect not only for the way our uniformed services are managed, but also for the dedicated and courageous men and women who have and are serving our county honorably. It may appear that I dislike controlled-access systems. I don't. There is nothing to detest since organizational forms are inert. People determine how best to organize their collective endeavors. I simply want to demonstrate that there is another even more effective option available to us for running our social institutions besides the top down hierarchy. Our decisions on how to make that choice should be based on solid evidence and not on myths or misinformation.

Emerging leadership. Figure 6-1 provides a graphic portrayal of the four key interactive elements of the no bossing or shared leadership process. To fully appreciate the self-organizing dynamics of shared leadership one needs to recall the difference between control and order and between machines and biological entities as discussed in Chapter Three.

Let's begin with the emerging leaders' element of the model. As is the case with all of our innate drives, leadership qualities are partly genetic and partly gained through life experiences. Hence, we all have leadership potential to one degree or another. For example, some of us may be more extraverted, conscientious, and open minded than our colleagues.

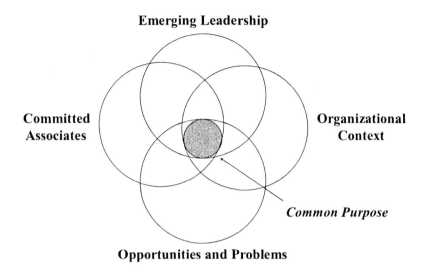

Figure 6-1. Elements of Shared Leadership

The same applies to our talents. One person may be naturally inclined for instant action, continuous learning, going for the gold instead of being satisfied with average results, or seeking meaningful connections in the world around them, while others may have completely different innate tendencies. What we all need to do is to discover what our natural predispositions are and put them to productive use. Unfortunately, countless people are more concerned with overcoming their deficiencies rather than leveraging their inherited abilities.

Unsurprisingly, leadership development follows personal growth. It is a progression whereby individuals with different traits and experiences will emerge to orchestrate activities in diverse situations. As mentioned before, no one person has the capacity to be an effective leader under all circumstances.

Fundamentally, from an evolutionary perspective, individuals with the "right stuff" (talent, skills, and know-how) attract other peoples' attention at appropriate occasions. Therefore, everyone needs to be prepared to take the lead when a fitting situation presents itself. In fact, members of an overt self-organizing group will look for and expect to receive advice and guidance from individuals who have expertise or experience in a particular area depending on the situation.

Committed associates. This leads us to the committed associates' component of the model. Recollect that one of our self-centered innate drives motivates us to mind read and generally keep track of the behavior of others. Thus, group members have a predictable inclination to evaluate who has the right stuff (and under what conditions) in helping to achieve reciprocally beneficial goals. Specifically, this means that the associates (as opposed to employees or followers) are constantly observing and categorizing the actions and reactions of their colleagues in dissimilar circumstances.

People look for unique qualities in each member that can be leveraged for the benefit of the entire group. In essence, they are continuously on the lookout for voluntarily engaging in the best possible opportunities that are mutually useful to all concerned. One can now comprehend why diverse sets of individuals outperform those that are more homogeneous and why everyone has the capacity and prospect to assume the lead at least occasionally. Further, individual status is derived from activities that attract others and, therefore, it's not absolute or permanent. So, as conditions and needs change, so can an individual's status as a prospective situational leader.

The significance of this is that in a shared-access system associates never relinquish their autonomy or surrender their personal powers, even temporarily, under any circumstances. At the same time, however, every member also accepts full responsibility and accountability for the success or failure of the clan as a whole. There can't be any compromises both from a personal as well as from an organizational perspective.

As is the case with individuals needing to be prepared to take the lead, everyone in an overt self-organizing system should also be cognizant of their associates' abilities in order to know who to turn to under specific conditions. No one should ever hesitate or be reluctant to ask for appropriate support. It is also important that associates continuously pursue personal development individually and in teams. After all, self-organization is about commitment and not about compliance. Each person knows when to take the lead and when to follow.

Opportunities and problems. The focus on opportunities or problems is the third element of the model. Fundamentally, what this suggests is that without an identified organizational opportunity to track, or a specific problem to solve, there is no need for leadership. In a shared-access system every member is constantly trying to discover new opportunities and to detect emergent problems that need attention (the focal point of the next chapter). These situations may be first investigated independently or immediately brought to the attention of other associates. It all depends on the potential dimensions and affect the situation may have on the enterprise.

Essentially, it is the responsibility of each group member to explore any positive or negative state of affairs that they happen to encounter. If they uncover a possible worthwhile new undertaking they can initially scrutinize it on their own or, from the start, solicit support from other interested people. In any case, once sufficient individuals are convinced that a project is worth pursuing, the associate who made the original discovery usually will assume the lead role in the venture if he or she feels that they have the right qualifications and there are enough other people willing to support the effort. Thus, dynamic order develops around the project from start to finish.

The course of action is founded on voluntary cooperation and commitment rather than compliance. This is an extremely important difference between no bossing leadership and leadership based on position power. No matter how benevolent, an appointed person in charge is rarely able to attain commitment from his or her followers since they mainly depend on reward and coercive power (actual or perceived) in gaining and holding people's attention. They seldom encounter situations where their known expertise and established relationships match perfectly and generate genuine commitment. Therefore, appointed leadership is mostly about the attainment of compliance (control) instead of commitment (order). In the process, effectiveness and efficiency suffer.

Organizational context. Organizational context is the fourth element depicted in Figure 6-1. Emergent leadership is seldom officially recognized and sanctioned within a controlled-access system. It is always present but, like a black market, it functions in the shadows or underground. As a clandestine operation there are no assurances whether the informal leadership supports, undermines, or simply stays neutral when it comes to formally declared policies and goals. Simply put, the realizations of the full benefits of shared leadership are slim to impossible to attain without the entire complement of self-organizing principles (discussed in Chapter Four) being in place. Hence, true situational leadership can realistically only be practiced in a shared-access organizational context.

Common purpose. Finally, as one can see, a common purpose is the central core that holds the entire shared leadership process together. It's the nucleus around which the four key elements revolve concurrently in a complementary and dynamic manner. Without *agreed upon* overall organizational intentions the framework, for all intents and purposes, falls apart.

For people lacking common purpose there is no need for expert advice or commitment from anyone since opportunities and problems encountered have no mutual appeal. It is similar to a "country club" environment. Everyone is out to have a good time but only for his or her own amusement. There is no need for unrestrained trust and reciprocity. Consequently, a common purpose is just as vital to the shared leadership process as are the four main elements.

In the final analysis, every part of the model works together simultaneously as is the case with all aspects of any self-organizing entity. Its dynamics are founded on commitment, which support the maintenance of high-sustained levels of social capital and the sharing of tacit knowledge. As I suggested at the beginning of the chapter, true leadership is all about:

Helping others to initiate or participate in worthwhile activities that they are either not aware of or are hesitant to take action on their own, which would benefit everyone involved.

6. TWO BRIEF ILLUSTRATIONS

Rowe Furniture Company is an excellent example of a classic controlled-access organization switching to a shared-access mode of operation and, in the process, adopting no bossing leadership.[10] Located in western Virginia's Appalachian foothills, Rowe had been run like a typical assembly-line sweatshop for more than 40 years producing standard quality furniture for retailers around the country. Suddenly in the mid-1990s, furniture buyers wanted custom-designed furniture and they demanded that the changeover be made within 90 days.

The firm immediately hired a new head of manufacturing to quickly develop a "hyperefficient assembly process." The new chief, however, instead of developing a faster and more efficient assembly line, discarded it completely. Most supervisory positions vanished with the assembly line and 500 workers were organized into teams or cells. Each product line of the company was assigned to a particular team that was also responsible for developing its own processes and procedures. In addition, the teams were given complete access to all the pertinent information—orders, output, quality, and productivity—they needed in order to do their work properly.

As one might guess, ambiguity and disbelief were widespread, but within weeks after everyone became accustomed to shared leadership, productivity and quality rose beyond all expectations. For instance, orders were filled within 30 days and subsequently in only 10 days—a feat unheard of in an industry where deliveries could take as long as six months. It's remarkable what people can accomplish with no bossing leadership. Better yet, not all the examples of shared leadership are found in high tech industries.

Another example of no bossing leadership can be found in a well functioning restaurant. Few people pay a lot of attention to the fast paced activities that take place in an eatery in response to orders taken from customers as long as they are served in a reasonable length of time. My wife and I have a favorite restaurant that we visit occasionally for late breakfast on Sundays. Like most individuals, I also had failed to closely observe the "behind the scenes behavior" in the restaurant that we've frequented for years until just recently.

One Saturday morning, waiting for a callback from our veterinarian, I decided to stop at our favorite breakfast place for a cup of coffee to kill some time. Sitting at the counter I was perfectly situated to see the interactions among the cooks in the kitchen, amid the servers going back and forth to pick up their orders, and between the cooks and the servers. What was most impressive was that there was no boss issuing any orders whatsoever. Everyone knew what needed to be done and went about carrying out their assignments very diligently and cooperatively. What was even more amazing was that the restaurant was filled to capacity and people were waiting to be seated.

Did everything go perfectly? Of course not. For instance, there was a rookie waiter who occasionally asked for help and who also received periodic unsolicited coaching from the seasoned staff. Further, the cooks were intermittently asked by the servers to make distinctions between different orders, to change some orders or to fill special requests. Not once, however, did anyone lose their temper or make an off-handed remark. Instead, there was constant laughter as people cracked jokes and occasionally made fun of each other while being very focused on what they were doing.

What was truly remarkable was how different people took the lead. One moment an individual would be asked for advice or they would provide it without being asked. Moments later the same attendant or cook would reverse roles without missing a beat. That is, at one time a cook would offer some advice to a server and shortly thereafter she would point out something to the man in the kitchen that would provide mutual benefits for all concerned.

It finally occurred to me that the reason there was no need for a boss was very simple. Everyone involved had a common purpose to get the food to the customer as quickly and cordially as possible. It was a classic win-win situation. A supervisor would only have gotten in the way and slowed down the whole process.

Given the proper organizational context (shared-access) no bossing leadership is the best option. If it can work in a restaurant, it certainly can work in most other places. In the next chapter I will delineate in detail how to pursue new opportunities and solve pressing problems within shared-access systems.

Chapter 7

RELENTLESSLY PURSUING OPPORTUNITIES

"It's not in my job description!" or "It's not my responsibility!" are frequently heard comments in controlled-access systems. That's because most lower ranking individuals believe that the assigned leaders and the authority system in general define the rules and limits of an enterprise and, as a result, are also responsible for its effectiveness. Consequently, when an average worker encounters a possible opportunity or problem, he or she usually ignores it rather than generating a solution or following up on a lead.

Dependency then, is a serious problem in controlled-access environments since people and groups are seldom allowed to make independent decisions or practice self-control. As a result, members of hierarchical organizations, to one degree or another, function under assumptions that encourage immature behavior, severely limiting their deliberate pursuit of opportunities.

When people have little power, they may begin to act in unusual and trivial ways. For example, they can become extremely regulation oriented and controlling to the point of over-managing everything they are required to do. I saw vivid illustrations of that behavior years ago on my visits to the former Soviet Union, especially when dealing with their customs officials. Every low ranking administrator seemed to take deliberate pleasure in scrutinizing your documents and belongings incessantly making sure that you were extremely frustrated and annoyed before they placed their precious stamp of approval on your documents.

Shared-access enterprises, on the other hand, not only purge most of the negative psychological tensions present in hierarchies by helping to balance the expression of our innate drives, but they are also, by design, suitably geared for dealing with today's complex and constantly changing global environment. As mentioned previously, ceaseless efforts to use linear and predictable methods to manage non-linear surroundings make little sense and are self-defeating. Thus, since current organizations must operate within a relentlessly shifting, information-rich and multi-faceted setting, they need to be exceedingly adaptable and resourceful in order to prosper.

Accordingly, this chapter introduces an integrated framework that can provide an organization the capacity to properly evaluate and pursue any of the opportunities and problems appearing on their radar screens daily. In order to accomplish that, I will first present a model for sustained individual and organizational learning capable of matching whatever complexity one's environment presents. I will conclude by proposing a multifaceted complementary scheme designed to help maintain dynamic order of the shared-access system.

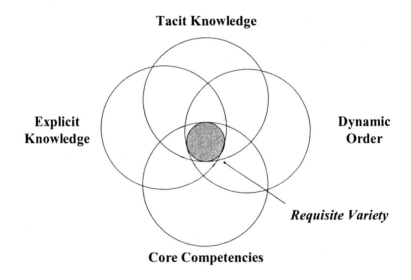

Figure 7-1. Pursuing Opportunities

Figure 7-1 portrays the key components of my proposed interactive framework for maximizing the pursuit of opportunities and for minimizing the surprise effects of unanticipated problems. Keep in mind that without the use of the full complement of overt self-organizing principles discussed in

Chapter Five, the application of the model is relatively ineffective. Before the scheme can be put into appropriate use an organization needs to have developed relatively high levels of social capital. That, of course, includes providing individuals a great deal of "responsible" autonomy, having a shared identity supported by interdependent face-to-face relationships, pursuing challenging mutually beneficial aspirations, maintaining dynamic alignment through shared leadership, and in the process allowing peoples' innate drives to be expressed in a balanced manner.

As are all the models incorporated into this book, Pursuing Opportunities is also vibrant and interdependent. Thus, if one part of the system is not up to speed the entire arrangement is degraded to a degree. This is another vivid example of why systems thinking (part of the Dynamic Alignment Principle) is so essential when we deal with any kind of living entity, such as a person or a social group.

1. ORGANIZATIONAL KNOWLEDGE

In examining the various elements of Figure 7-1 and their significance, begin with *requisite variety* since it is the core of the structure. The law of requisite variety is a systems theory concept originated by W.R. Ashby in the early 1950s. He pointed out that if a system is to continue to exist properly it must be able to match whatever complexity its environment presents to it.[1]

Obviously, being capable of responding to all environmental situations on a one-to-one rather than one-to-many basis is the ultimate goal in managing requisite variety. For example, a team (pick your favorite team sport) preparing to meet one of its adversaries and expecting to win must be capable of matching both the offensive and defensive schemes of the opponent—have requisite variety. That is, the team must meet an array of problems with an equal variety of solutions.

Such a feat is impossible in a controlled-access setting since most everything is directed and controlled from the top down. Therefore, hierarchies develop policies and procedures founded on past incidents that everyone is supposed to adhere to diligently. In doing so, they are trying to deal with future events hoping that history will, in effect, repeat itself. Reacting to environmental conditions on a one-to-many basis (a boss making decisions for the subordinates) *may* have been sufficient in the more stable surroundings of the past but is not a smart strategy for the current unpredictable and information-rich world.

A shared-access framework, on the other hand, is designed to respond to environmental complexity on a one-to-one basis as much as possible. Each member of the clan is responsible, accountable and capable of taking action either on his or her own or with assistance of other interested individuals instantly as conditions warrant. There are no built in delays due to disinterest or having to run to management to get appropriate authorization. Everything is set up for real-time action and reaction.

Information and knowledge are the keys to maintaining requisite variety. Therefore, organizations that are better able to acquire, share, and leverage all aspects of the world that surrounds them will prosper now and in the future. How ironic. As is the case with the informal self-organizing side of our institutions, we have known the importance of requisite variety for decades yet most enterprises keep on ignoring it. Is it a wonder that so many organizations, large and small, have such a high failure rate? As one can readily observe, the other four components of Figure 7-1 combined, generate and sustain the requisite variety of an institution.

2. UNCONNECTED KNOW-HOW

As mentioned in Chapter Two, unrelated or tacit knowledge is acquired through first hand experiences and by interacting with more knowledgeable people and groups. It includes ideas and generalizations at the individual level. Tacit knowledge, because it is unrelated to specific facts and events, can't be found in databases, documents, books, files, libraries, or the Internet. Thus, it can only be partially shared orally and it can't be codified or transmitted by formal means. Also, tacit knowledge must be allowed to emerge. It can't be forced or supervised out of people since nobody is fully aware of all the disparate knowledge that they possess.

We also know today that many of the neural memory networks involved in implicit learning have evolved separately from what is accessible by the conscious brain. As the distinguished neuroscientist Joseph LeDoux stipulates:

Each of us has his or her own style of walking, talking, and thinking...We notice things that some others ignore, and ignore things that some people notice...The extent to which we are calm and collected, or emotionally reactive, when things go awry...as are the logical paths and illogical leaps of thought we have. These and many other aspects of mind and behavior are expressed so automatically, so implicitly, that they may be unchangeable, perhaps innate. But we should not overlook the crucial role of experience, which is to say of learning and memory, in establishing and maintaining them.[2]

Our worldviews. In essence, everyone, from the time that they are born to the time they come to the end of their journey on earth, is continuously exposed to all sorts of values, facts, perceptions, and events. This is how we develop our so-called *weltanschauung* or *worldview* in combination with our genetic predispositions. Without this repertoire of unconnected know-how we would not be able to suitably categorize people, places, and events instantaneously so that we can take appropriate action when we encounter them. We couldn't survive a day without tacit knowledge. Can you imagine thinking everything through from start to finish including getting out of bed, brushing teeth, riding a bicycle, or writing a letter?

It should be clear now why we can never completely access and articulate our worldview that is based on our experiences, assumptions, perceptions, values, fears and so on. For the same reasons it's not possible to *directly* transfer our unrelated knowledge to other people and groups by such means as seminars, training manuals and e-mails. For example, when was the last time anyone learned to ride a bicycle by reading an instruction manual? We all know that the only way to learn to ride a bike is to get on one and experience what it takes to stay on it.

Every person is similar in a very general way to other human beings. For instance, we all have similar basic physical and mental characteristics. At the same time, however, we are also quite different from one another in our appearance as well as frame of mind. What this means is that each individual acquires expertise in his or her own unique way and applies it in a similar fashion. Therefore, as stipulated in the Chapter Two, tacit knowledge is a very dynamic and pliable resource.

The wellspring of innovations. It's important to keep in mind that the wellspring of all new ideas is tacit knowledge. Organizations need to find ways that allow unrelated know-how to surface so that it can be made explicit and put to productive use. Because tacit knowledge emerges voluntarily it can be applied both negatively and positively (from an organizational perspective).

In a controlled-access institution a great deal of the voluntary activity and knowledge sharing is pushed underground and there are no accurate means to predict or control how that knowledge will be put to "unrestrained" use. It all depends on how goals are selected and pursued to the satisfaction of everyone concerned.

Quite the opposite is true in a shared-access system. Since all members are considered to be partners (each recognized for making some type of an investment in the enterprise including such things as special abilities, patents, processes, capital, etc.), it's to their and the organization's advantage to constantly be on the lookout for new opportunities and potential problems. That's the primary difference between committed associates and employees complying with directives. One group genuinely cares about the success of a venture while the other set of people usually just puts in their required time.

Activation of unrelated knowledge. Tacit knowledge comes to the fore only when new opportunities or problems are encountered. For example, as an individual or a team in a shared-access system thinks of a more effective way to promote a product, sees a competitor about to enter their most lucrative market or senses a new way to augment one of the organization's core competencies (defined shortly) they immediately leap into action either on their own or with appropriate support from others. In analyzing the situation and reaching for alternative solutions, unrelated knowledge begins to surface and is then, in a variety of ways, coupled to the emerging options. Also, the more intensely tacit knowledge is shared, the more innovative and valuable will be its focused applications (Please see Figure 7-2 for a graphic depiction of this dynamic process). The process is voluntary because all concerned have a personal stake in it.

Recall the discussion of life's common purpose in Chapter Three— survive long enough in order to be able to pass on the genes and culture to the next generation. This means that we only get seriously involved in an event if the *perceived outcome* may impact our life's common purpose beneficially.

That is, when faced either with a positive or a negative novel situation we innately reach into our "bag" full of unconnected know-how and try to weave some of that knowledge together in order to solve a problem or take advantage of an opportunity where we are a key player. This is another reason why a *genuine* common vision (part of the Challenging Aspirations Principle) is so vital for the successful operation of a shared-access clan and the sharing of tacit knowledge.

Fundamentally, tacit knowledge derives its potency from the fact that it is instantly accessible, practical, and malleable given the right circumstances. It is also the starting point for all new discoveries. That is the useful side of unrelated knowledge.

There, of course, is also a down side to this seldom-tapped organizational resource. Some people accumulate all sorts of strange facts, values, assumptions, and ideas in the course of their lives. Consequently, when they reach into their bag of tacit tricks what emerges may be unique but quite useless. That is another reason why considerable time must be spent in determining who should be invited to join a shared-access institution.

Practices for leveraging tacit knowledge. The above are the basic facts about tacit knowledge. Are there specific practices that can be used to enhance the emergence of unconnected know-how in an organizational setting? Certainly. Clearly, from a macro perspective, a fully developed shared-access system with its complement of principles supporting overt self-organization is the best way to draw tacit knowledge to the surface. However, there are additional means that can be used to further augment the "mining" and sharing of tacit knowledge.

For starters, the physical layout of an organization has a significant impact on how often and intensely unrelated knowledge is tapped into. Recollect that the Shared Identity Principle prescribes as much face-to-face or line-of-sight interaction among clan members as possible. This obviously implies that people who need to work together shouldn't be located on different floors or in separate buildings. Further, if cubicles are used for limited privacy the partitions should not be any higher than four feet, topped by two feet of glass, giving associates good all around visibility yet lessening the noise factor of informal chats and telephone conversations.

Additionally, the entrances to the cubicles should face an open area furnished with tables and chairs. This type of an arrangement is necessary to house impromptu meetings among individuals and teams. There should also be conference rooms available for groups of people to meet in when they are engaged in lengthy deliberations requiring privacy (with clients for instance) or when walls are needed to post suggestions on. Finally, there should be ample space where individuals can occasionally go to work in isolation away from all the daily activities.

These are just some very general suggestions. Clearly, every organization needs to find its own unique ways to assure that the physical layout supports face-to-face interactions as much as possible. However, I need to provide a note of caution. It is absolutely essential that any arrangement selected doesn't grant certain individuals larger or more desired space.

There is no place for special privileges in a shared-access system, which automatically begins to hamper tacit knowledge sharing. It also opens the door for a hierarchy to begin to creep in. For example, if cubicles are used some of them should not be more spacious, have higher partitions or be deliberately isolated from the others. Remember, status in a self-organizing environment is founded on expertise and accomplishments, not on rank.

Now let us take a brief look at some additional means that can be used to boost unconnected know-how sharing. First, clan members need to educate and re-educate themselves on the criticality of maintaining close and meaningful face-to-face interactions with one another. Next, everyone should be clear about the fact that pleasing the customer takes precedence over all other activities. This means that day-to-day activities, projects and other commitments must be completed or receive adequate consideration before time is devoted to future ventures. Naturally, unexpected events that threaten the viability of an organization are the exception to the rule and must be given immediate attention.

Lastly, there are certain other processes that can be employed to leverage tacit knowledge by individuals, teams and the clan as a whole. At the individual level (adhering to the Individual Autonomy Principle) every associate should maintain informal ties internally and externally with experts in related fields, periodically have personal contact with customers (especially non-marketers), take time to visit suppliers, and generally rub elbows with any person or entity that may be a source for new emerging ideas.

Further, people can experiment with new concepts, ravenously read journals in both related and unrelated fields, and reflect on things or processes that presently may seem unfeasible but that would be tremendously advantageous if means to achieve them could be discovered. Teams throughout an enterprise can also use similar practices to enhance tacit knowledge development and application.

At the organizational level unconnected know-how sharing can take several forms. First, periodic clan-wide meetings can be held to familiarize all members with the experiments, new ideas, concepts, and processes that are being discussed or seriously investigated. Second, occasional social events may be scheduled where people can maintain their relationships with associates they do not work with routinely.

Third, an organization should develop and maintain a practical and easily accessible system where "raw" ideas can be posted for incubation and for initiation of new collaborative efforts. Information technology can be of help with this matter. It must be remembered, however, that such a system, no matter how sophisticated, can never replace the need for face-to-face interactions when it comes to the sharing of unconnected know-how.

It may appear from the above that I'm against all forms of virtual networks and teams. Absolutely not. Technology should be used as best as possible to *support* any form of collaboration. However, we should never forget that organizations are made up of human beings. Accordingly, if members of an institution seldom or never have an occasion to go face-to-face with one another, they will be unable to draw on the physiological benefits derived from close contact that are extremely important for the development of high levels of trust and the sharing of tacit knowledge. Hence, virtual teams need to have ample opportunities to periodically meet in person.

3.   ACCESSING WHAT IS KNOWN

Explicit knowledge consists of data and information that has been codified or formally defined. It is a static resource. Formalized knowledge can be accessed by such means as education, training, books, journals and the Internet among others. Although explicit knowledge is not the wellspring of new concepts it is very important for three reasons. First, it is the foundation for all recognized day-to-day activities. That is, before anything (new process, new technology, new drug, etc.) can be put to productive use it must first be made explicit.

Second, data and information can be managed, whereas tacit knowledge can't. For instance, explicit knowledge can be stored, manipulated, copied, and transferred. It can also be reapplied. Finally, explicit knowledge (new and old) triggers or stimulates the development of new ideas and innovations. For example, a person reading a journal, attending a seminar, or working with a software program may all of a sudden have a revelation about something that has not been tried before but could improve some activity or technology considerably. Significant or trivial, we all have had those moments in our lives.

Figure 7-2 portrays the dynamic relationships between individuals sharing tacit and explicit knowledge as they develop new innovative solutions (new emergent explicit knowledge) for identified problems or opportunities. Notice how the three circles overlap depicting how the tacit and explicit knowledge of the persons collaborating in the process concurrently surfaces and expands since they are both teachers and learners. At the same time new explicit knowledge surfaces as solutions are developed, this in turn, further enlarges the tacit and explicit knowledge repertoire of the participants. It's a win-win situation for both the partakers and the organization as a whole.

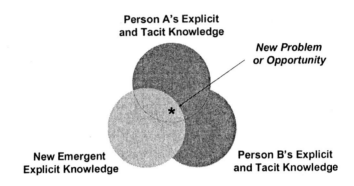

Figure 7-2. Emergent Explicit Knowledge

It is crucial in the Knowledge Age that organizations maintain an *integrated database* containing all the relevant internal and external information vital to the operation of an enterprise and its associated industry or industries. What is absolutely essential is that such a centralized intellectual asset repository be extremely easy to use and accessible to all members of an institution.

The central database also needs to be fully integrated with all the pertinent information systems throughout an organization. If it's not, all the information within an organization stored in multiple files will seldom be in sync, up-to-date, employ standard terminology, or easily available to everyone. Limiting access to a small number of individuals when there is an integrated system has a similar effect.

Security is a legitimate concern but it can be appropriately managed without limiting access to critical information to only a few select people. After all, in a shared-access system we are dealing with highly selected people or partners, not employees who, like mercenaries, are ready to accommodate the highest bidder. Owners rarely compromise the interests of their own hard earned assets.

One should bear in mind that information is the lifeblood of a self-organizing system. By limiting the flow of information one is, in effect, putting a tourniquet around key parts of an organization restraining or, in the long run, choking off their effectiveness. The same is true if there is a wide-open integrated database that is complicated, time consuming and confusing to access. People will simply ignore such a system and find other ways to satisfy their information needs.

Thus, information technology, properly applied, can be of tremendous help in managing explicit knowledge. Unlike other finite resources (such as raw materials, labor, and monetary assets), information and intellectual capital in general are infinite resources. Being a limitless commodity means that the more knowledge is shared and manipulated, the faster and larger it grows. Consequently, besides employing a high tech integrated data system that is human friendly, an organization also needs to have a robust knowledge-sharing culture. That is another reason why an institution needs to have developed high levels of social capital before they can get serious about applying all sorts of leading-edge communications hardware and software.

So, what are some of the more important information sources that should be included in an organizational database? Clearly, every institution has its own unique explicit knowledge requirements. There are, however, certain universal categories that need to be commonly known and tracked. To begin with, everyone in a clan should have intimate knowledge of every member's talents, skills and experience. How else will people and teams know exactly who to contact when faced with a unique problem or when pursuing newly discovered opportunities.

Yes, in a shared-access system there are continuous face-to-face interactions and, therefore, everyone has a general idea about everybody else's backgrounds. Unfortunately, people can only retain limited amounts of detail. Also, if the clan is a member of a large organization composed of numerous other small relatively autonomous groups, the matter becomes even more complicated.

Next, every member should be very familiar with the core competencies of their venture. I will discuss the importance of core competencies shortly but for the moment let me simply say that they can be referred to as the "talents" of an organization. Hence, if people are not sure what those special capabilities are they can't realistically look for and identify opportunities that the clan may want to pursue. Just as individuals must first identify what their abilities are before they can apply them productively, the same holds true for organizations. To make sense, opportunities have got to be tied to capabilities.

Further, as people work on various tasks or are developing plans for new ventures, they should be able to reference historical files of prior organizational activities. That is, it is not very wise to "reinvent the wheel" when you don't have to every time another job is started. Therefore, the central repository should contain fairly detailed records of projects that have been completed. At a minimum, these project files should show what the initial plans were, what actually transpired, and the lessons learned.

Finally, the database should also hold or be linked to five other more general sources. First, for convenience, there should be direct links to vital external databases dealing with subjects related to the core competencies of the institution. Second, there need to be files providing wide-ranging information about the organization's suppliers and customers. Third, there should be links to the major professional associations recognized for their world-class efforts in areas pertinent to the success of the enterprise. Fourth, it is crucial that the central repository contain sufficient information about organizational competitors and potential contenders. Finally, clan members should have a realistic and impartial view of their company's reputation compiled from a variety of independent external sources.

4.   ORGANIZATIONAL TALENTS

As suggested earlier, core competencies are the talents of an enterprise. I continue to be amazed in my discussions with corporate leaders and MBA students how few of them understand what core competencies are and their significance to the success of an institution. Even in some cases when an individual can roughly define what constitutes a core competency they have great difficulty in specifying what the talents of their own company are. Most people usually relate core competencies to an organization's products or services. How anyone can assume that they will be able to realistically pursue opportunities without first knowing what their firm's talents are is difficult for me to fathom.

Prahalad and Hamel are the originators of the concept of organizational core competencies.[3] They define these fundamental institutional talents as "the collective learning in organizations, especially how to coordinate diverse production skills and integrate multiple streams of technologies." They also point out that "unlike physical assets, which deteriorate over time, competencies are enhanced as they are applied and shared." In effect, improved and new products and services are continually derived from leading-edge core competencies

Organizational talents can be categorized into three general areas: proficiency in certain technologies, coordination or process skills, and special abilities in developing and maintaining external relationships or networks.[4] Thus, an enterprise that pays close attention to its core competencies will be much more responsive to new opportunities than an institution steadfastly locked into its products and services.[5] This is precisely why I strongly recommend that shared-access systems be organized around core competencies instead of functional areas or end products.

It should be quite apparent that in the Knowledge Age organizational viability and resilience is primarily dependent on the rate and intensity with which tacit knowledge is shared. However, as stipulated before, for unconnected know-how to emerge the people involved need to have a common cause to rally around. That's why core competencies should be the primary focal point for institutions seeking both short- and long-term opportunities for improving organizational effectiveness. Keeping the spotlight on core competencies makes it easier for people to ask the right questions leading to the continuous development of new and enhanced products and services.

Moreover, keeping a firm eye on institutional talents facilitates the development of appropriate scenarios in anticipating the future. Thus, the same methods and systems I've proposed for leveraging tacit and explicit knowledge can be used as well in continuously upgrading the core competencies in preventing a devastating organizational disease called "core rigidities."

5.   DYNAMIC ORDER

The final piece of the requisite variety puzzle comes under the heading of "Dynamic Order." It could just as well be called, "What's Happening and How Are We All Doing?" In any case, because of the significance of the dynamic order component to the Pursuing Opportunities System, I've developed a separate model to describe the multifaceted activities that are a vital part of that process. Figure 7-3 depicts a general framework that an organization should develop and maintain in order to keep track of all its activities and to enhance its capability to rapidly respond to opportunities and problems.

Fundamentally, if an overt self-organizing entity can't provide its members and teams real-time information as to the status of all its activities and interactions, it may begin to break up into more manageable sub-components. What this means is that limiting the size of the enterprise to 150 people or less and maintaining close face-to-face relationships might not always be sufficient to prevent the eventual fragmentation of a shared-access system.

Individuals and teams, for instance, may start to drift away from a common vision and begin to inadvertently modify their self-reference when they have a limited view as to what everybody else is doing and how well they are meeting their commitments. Thus, it helps to have a formal system that allows everyone to have a comprehensive view of all the activities that are taking place in an organization.

Two important points need to be kept in mind. First, the "formalized" process is designed to not only help people stay on track but also to be a viable aid for decision-making. Hence, it must be convenient to use and kept up-to-date by *all* clan members. This means that the maintenance of the system cannot be made the *sole* responsibility of an individual, team or department. As soon as that takes place I can guarantee that the people will slowly but surely drift away from it. Second, such a system doesn't replace but rather firmly supports a very interdependent and knowledge-sharing culture that generates the requisite variety necessary for effectively responding to continuous environmental changes.

Figure 7-3 portrays four key elements for the development and maintenance of dynamic order in a shared-access system. Again, as is the case with all the models in this book, all components of the system need to be fully up and running before optimum benefits can be derived from the arrangement. Further, we need to recall that dynamic order has nothing to do with control (a static concept) as discussed in Chapter Four.

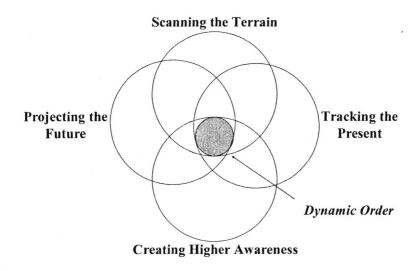

Scanning the Terrain

Projecting the
Future

Tracking the
Present

Dynamic Order

Creating Higher Awareness

Figure 7-3. Maintaining Dynamic Order

Scanning the terrain. Clearly, dissimilar environmental conditions impose different demands but, at the same time, offer special opportunities for an organization. In order for an enterprise to be cognizant of these changing states it needs to continuously gather data from its environment and convert the collected data into meaningful information. That information is then used for day-to-day decision-making and for amending or altering long-range plans and programs.

Scanning the "terrain" gives the appearance of being a relatively uncomplicated process. Unfortunately, it's not. That is probably why most institutions fail to do an adequate job in scrutinizing the environment and worse, some ignore it altogether. Keeping accurate track of changing global conditions entails overcoming two major obstacles. The first one is the most obvious.

The state of affairs around the world changes by the minute. So, it is not a question of time if some event is going to be missed but rather how many episodes will fail to be detected and analyzed even when tracked with unlimited resources. An infinite ever-churning sea of visible and hidden information surrounds us. Hence, it is impossible to be aware of all the global transformations (pertinent and otherwise) that may impact us and we must learn how to make decisions under uncertainty. That is, we need to carefully determine what information sources should be routinely tapped and what processes can be used to search the environment for the less obvious facts and expert observations.

The second hurdle involves individual interpretations. Recall the "worldview" aspect of tacit knowledge I discussed earlier in the chapter. What is significant about our worldviews or perceptions is that they are comprised of "screens" developed over a lifetime that we use to make sense of our surroundings. On balance, "the fundamental triad of higher brain functions is composed of perceptual categorizations, memory, and learning.... Perceptual categorization is generally necessary for memory, which is, after all, about previous categorization."[6] Learning, in turn, is dependent on categorization and memory that also provides us the ability to anticipate the future.

Consequently, we are born with an innate foundation for developing our worldviews and using that capacity for our actions and interactions for survival. That is the good news. The bad news is that nobody is capable of seeing an object or an event precisely the same way as another person. This poses an interesting dilemma for an organization. "Who decides what environmental data is pertinent to the enterprise and how should it be interpreted?" My answer to the above question is quite unconventional. As many clan members as possible should be involved in environmental data analysis.

My suggestion is based on the premise that the more perspectives are offered the more alternative courses of action can be considered in making the final decision. As pointed out in Chapter Five, consensus decision-making doesn't mean everyone's inputs will be acted upon. Rather, it denotes that all suggestions are thoroughly examined. Thus, effectively deciding what to scan and how to interpret the collected data presents a bigger problem for a controlled-access than a shared-access institution. In the former only a select few are permitted to make the key decisions whereas in the latter everyone is expected to air their observations.

Anticipating the future. Effective decision-making is the foundation for maintaining dynamic order and it's accomplished in two principal ways—rationally and intuitively. Let's first take a brief look at the rational side. Several decades ago Herbert A. Simon delineated that, fundamentally, decision-making consists of three interrelated steps, "(1) finding an occasion for making a decision, (2) finding possible courses of action, and (3) choosing among courses of action."[7] One more step needs to be added to make the process complete. It includes implementation of the selected course of action and the assessment of its actual effectiveness.[8]

As one can readily conclude, each of the four stages of decision-making is dependent not only on the magnitude and reliability of the information acquired through scanning, but also on the ability to anticipate the future reasonably well. That is, an organization not only needs *feedback* channels that portray the present state of its affairs but also reliable *feedforward* systems for predicting future outcomes or events.

For example, becoming aware of a problem or discovering an opportunity takes extensive environmental awareness (scanning). Identifying possible courses of action demands more in-depth research on the feasibility of the proposed options. Next, selecting the final option for implementation is dependent on further facts and figures in supporting its viability beyond the other alternatives. Steps two and three are reliant on the capability of people to "fairly consistently" forecast the outcomes of the option considered or (feedforward). Finally, once implemented, accurate information is needed to determine how well the chosen course of action is meeting expectations (feedback) so that appropriate steps can be taken to correct deviations or to make further improvements.

Rationally anticipating the future can take many forms. My favorite method is the use of a "crystal ball" with the help of a certified fortuneteller. You can't beat 100 percent guaranteed reliability! Seriously, for dealing with the increasing rate of change around the world (today even domestic players must take a global perspective in order to survive), scenario thinking and planning has gained widespread acceptance. Scenario thinking is especially suitable for forecasting in today's environment since the process is minimally dependent on historical events and data.

Fundamentally, scenario thinking forces people to stretch their minds by asking difficult questions and then developing contingency plans in response to the concerns raised. Some of the key questions that should be asked are:

- What would make our organization a greater success than we could possibly imagine?
- What would destroy our venture?
- What could possibly take place to change our enterprise fundamentally?[9]

In order to properly respond to these questions, organizational members need to do three things. First, they must find fitting sources of information that test their viewpoints and, at the same time, expand them. Second, their questions need to be challenged by dissimilar environmental contexts. For instance, people need to determine what the responses to the above questions would be if economic conditions improved significantly in the next ten years and, conversely, if the exact opposite would take place during the same time frame. Organizations essentially need to determine how best to survive under both favorable and unfavorable conditions.

Finally, scenario planning must be centered on the institution's core competencies unless members choose to acquire or develop brand new capabilities. Just like an individual, an organization needs to continuously focus on amplifying its talents rather than spending unwarranted resources on limited aptitudes. It makes little sense trying to cover all the bases. A better option is to team up with another entity that has the competencies that your venture lacks.

Anticipating the future intuitively is as important as or even more so than using any of the wide variety of rational schemes that have been devised by humans up to this point. Recent multidisciplinary research is beginning to make clear why that is the case. Fundamentally, it's again all about human nature. Our neurological framework evolved for survival on the African Savannah, not for extreme forms of rational computation.

Hence, compared to computers, we're terrible at crunching numbers but great at pattern recognition, such as anticipating outcomes based on just very limited observations of certain events. In effect, pattern detection takes place at a subconscious level. Further, research indicates that "gut feelings" or emotions initiate the decision-making process providing our rational side an initial list of possible future events. Lacking intuition a decision wouldn't get off the ground.

As Thomas A. Stewart has concluded:

> The most brilliant decisions tend to come from the gut. While that observation is not new, it is now backed by a growing body of research from economics, neurology, cognitive psychology, and other fields. What the science suggests is that intuition—or instinct, or hunch, or "learning without awareness," or whatever you want to call it—is a real form of knowledge. It may be none rational, ineffable, and not always easy to get in touch with, but it can process more information on a more sophisticated level than most of us ever dreamed. Psychologists now say that far from being the opposite of effective decision-making, intuition is indispensable from it. Without it we couldn't decide anything at all.[10]

It should now be apparent why in extremely unstable circumstances—like fighting a fire, dealing on the floor of a stock exchange, or in the middle of combat—all one can really depend on is intuition or tacit knowledge. Thus, by necessity, intuition is critical for creativity and the generation of innovative ideas. Hunches should never be ignored.

Creating higher awareness. Taking time out occasionally to reflect on the past and present is probably the most neglected practice by both people and organizations. As Gosling and Mintzberg indicate:

"Reflect" in Latin means to refold, which suggests that attention turns inward so that it can be turned outward. This means going beyond introspection. It means looking in so that you can better see out in order to perceive a familiar thing in a different way—a product as a service, maybe, or a customer as a partner.[11]

Gaining a higher awareness of the world around us, both individually and institutionally, is extremely beneficial yet many people consider it to be a misuse of valuable time and money.

I know of no other way, however, in gaining an understanding of how we are "truly" making progress and what is really important in our lives. Some of us need to experience a shocking event such as the devastation of war, a terminal illness taking the life of a loved one, or the horror of the attack on the World Trade Center on September 11th, 2001 before we take stock of our lives. It doesn't need to be that extreme in order for us to try to get out of the rut. That also applies to an organization as a whole.

New awareness levels are normally achieved through times set aside for reflection at two general levels—individual and organizational. Clearly, people need to stop occasionally to ponder what their true values and beliefs are; if they are pursuing worthwhile goals, and if they are currently involved with the right institution(s). In effect, one should ask, "What is really important in my life and am I living my life accordingly?" The key to success in this process is to be as honest with yourself as possible. That is, we need to sort out our assumptions from genuine facts.

A similar practice should be followed at the team and organizational levels. Here the fundamental questions that need to be periodically asked are: "How realistic is our common vision?" "Are we pursuing our goals as best as we can? Should we change direction completely?" As at the individual level, honesty is absolutely indispensable in conducting these exercises.

Accordingly, the use of dialogue, as opposed to debate or discussion, is the best choice of tools for an awareness workout. In a debate there are winners and losers and in a typical discussion some proposals will be accepted over others. Properly employed dialogue, however, takes everyone involved to a higher level of overall awareness. As stipulated by Peter Senge:

In a dialogue, a group explores complex difficult issues from many points of view. Individuals suspend their assumptions but they communicate their assumptions freely. The result is a free exploration that brings to the surface the full depth of people's experience and thought, and yet can move beyond their individual views.... Once people

see the participatory nature of their thoughts, they begin to separate
themselves from their thought. They begin to take a more creative, less
reactive, stance toward their thought.[12]

There are three fundamental ground rules for a dialogue:
- Suspension of assumptions. People typically take a position and defend it
  as do other participants in a discussion or debate. In a dialogue,
  assumptions behind varying interpretations of key issues are surfaced.
- Acting as colleagues. Everyone leaves his or her status or position at the
  door.
- Spirit of inquiry. People must be willing to explore the thinking behind
  their views, the deeper assumptions they hold, and the evidence they
  have that leads them to these views.

Essentially, the process is used to shed light on the fact that all of us, to
one degree or another, base our interpretations, assumptions, and actions on
very subjective reasoning. It is also quite fascinating that "the practice of
dialogue has been preserved in many 'primitive' cultures, such as that of the
American Indian, but it has been almost completely lost to modern society."
As suggested before, we have much to learn from our forgotten and ignored
past.

Tracking the present. The final component of the Maintaining Dynamic
Order Model is relatively uncomplicated but as vital to the process as the
other three interrelated elements. Providing *maximum visibility* to all
members of the clan of the internal and external activities that the
organization is involved in, is a significant feature of the module.

We are all familiar with the expression, "Out of sight, out of mind." That
phrase is equally applicable to a clan's multiple actions and interactions.
That is, as long as the organizational activities are observable, they usually
get the necessary attention. Conversely, when events or projects, for
whatever reason, drop off the radar screen, they are quickly forgotten and
ignored. The maintenance of face-to-face relationships alone is not sufficient
to eliminate this problem.

Therefore, a shared-access entity needs a tracking system for all of its
critical proceedings and assignments. Such a system can be either manual or
electronic as long as everybody benefits from it and helps to keep it current.
What is critical is that all key events be visibly tracked at three distinct
levels—individual, team, and the organization as a whole.

The reason for this is straightforward. An individual must demonstrate
what actions they have committed to and how far they have progressed in
their assignments. At the same time, people need to know what impact their
efforts are having on the success of the teams they are working with and the

clan as a whole so that they can continue to respond effectively. How else can individuals be *equitably* rewarded for their efforts? I will discuss the equitable (not equal) distribution of earnings in more detail shortly.

The same applies to team projects and activities. Teams need to show what they are involved in and their achievements to date. In addition, they need to have feedback with regards to the significance of their contributions to the success of the venture, which allows them to make necessary adjustments in their efforts and to be properly rewarded for their labors. Of course, the results of individual and team efforts are then compiled to indicate how and why the organization is progressing in its entirety towards agreed upon goals.

There are no secrets in an open self-organizing system including how members are rewarded. There are no "bosses" to make those determinations since all clan members are partners to one degree or another. Hence, everyone needs to understand what everybody else is doing and achieving both from an operational as well as an equitable compensation standpoint. Without such candidness, synergistic systems thinking and high levels of voluntary collaboration would be impossible to attain.

Consequently, people need to have free access not only to performance data, but also to financial records. As partners in the venture, everyone needs to be involved in determining how much of the surplus is reinvested in the enterprise and how much is distributed to its members. That means that during good years individual and team rewards can be relatively high unless a decision is made to reinvest the excess income. As expected, the reverse is true during lean periods.

It's been well demonstrated that giving all members of an organization significant equity ownership (where the equity potential is considerably higher than their salary) increases people's contributions and innovation more than the financial potential may imply.[13] I must stress again that equitable distribution of an institution's surplus to its partners has nothing in common with "equal" allocation of rewards. Rather, it means that gains are shared based on individual and team contributions to the overall institutional efforts. In an "open book" environment few people have trouble understanding and accepting what equitable compensation entails.

I need to add a few more comments about data visibility. As mentioned before, the tracking system can be either manual or electronic as long as the displays are visible and up-to-date. Therefore, making the information accessible only on the organization's computer network is not sufficient. Individual and team activities need to be observable at work areas so that people walking around can quickly get an idea of what is going on and how well things are progressing.

Also, clan members will usually be participating in several events or team projects at a time and need to know how well they are meeting their commitments, what undertaking they may want to join next, or who can use some additional help to meet their goals. Thus, the more individuals and teams are aware that people around them care and pay attention to what they are doing, the more pride they will take in their assignments. Further, activity displays needn't be very sophisticated or high tech. In fact, the simpler they are the easier they are to read as long as they show most of the relevant information. Please see Appendix B for an uncomplicated example.

Visibility supports circular causality, which is the basis for self-organization and the sharing of tacit knowledge. Being cognizant of other associates' activities in a shared-access system has nothing to do with "spying" on people or controlling others, as it may be perceived in a hierarchical enterprise. Instead, it is all about unadulterated teamwork.

Finally, it helps to have a location where all the data and information tracked by the clan is centrally displayed. Such an "operations center" provides a convenient way for individuals and teams to quickly bring themselves up to speed as to the latest developments throughout the organization. It is also an appropriate place to hold planning sessions and to brief trusted customers, suppliers, and other key external network participants.

It is quite evident that relentlessly pursuing opportunities and maintaining dynamic order is by and large based on persistent systems thinking. Systems thinking is process thinking, which encourages us to share ideas, experiences, and knowledge culminating in new higher-level perspectives for all involved. It is about self-reliant autonomous individuals forming voluntary networks because they realize that interdependence and teamwork provide a much greater chance for success than going it alone. As Kevin Kelly makes clear:

> "Autonomous" means that each member reacts individually according to internal rules and the state of its local environment…These autonomous members are highly connected to each other, but not to a central hub. They thus form a peer network. Since there is no center of control, the management and heart of the system are said to be decentrally distributed within the system.[14]

In Chapter eight, the focus is on the actuation of the hidden triad of organizational success factors and the hidden assets of an organization.

Chapter 8

ACTUATING THE INVISIBLE TRIAD

In the 21st Century, knowledge is the key source for wealth creation. Therefore, in order to succeed, our social institutions need to abandon the Industrial Age mind-set and learn how to leverage the hidden triad of organizational success factors. We no longer can afford the luxury of continuing to ignore that humans have evolved to function quite well without all sorts of superimposed structures and motivational schemes. Hence, *unmanagement,* not the further refinements of hierarchies, will help us to better deal with the uncertainties, complexities, and perpetual change in the years to come.

Up to this point I've offered evidence of a number of critical but invisible elements present in all social settings. For instance, I've summarized some of the fundamental survival principles and genetic predispositions of humans. I've also shown that self-organization begins at the molecular level and extends to a person's contact with his or her immediate physical and social surroundings.

Further, I've stipulated that the more social capital an organization is capable of generating, the more it's able to achieve outcomes that would be unattainable without it or that could only be attained with additional resources.[1] Furthermore, I demonstrated that tacit knowledge must be allowed to emerge through voluntary collaboration or self-organization. It can't forced or managed out of people since they seldom are aware of exactly what unrelated knowledge they possess until confronted with a problem or an opportunity where they perceive themselves to be a key participant.[2]

In this final chapter, I'll display the remarkably close interdependent relationships between what I consider to be *the three most decisive organizational success dynamics—informal self-organizing networks, social capital, and tacit knowledge.* Knowing how to access and leverage these powerful invisible forces will give any organization a much better chance to succeed in today's turbulent global landscape.

Rather than attempting to dodge or ignore these irrepressible dynamics that take place in all social settings and push them underground, it's by far more beneficial to cultivate them openly. Hence, institutions that will develop shared-access work environments will not only be more productive in their endeavors but also more human friendly. After all, leveraging the invisible forces present within all social groups is not just meant to support formal organizational objectives but life in general.

1.   UNACCOUNTED FOR RESOURCES

In the previous chapter I indicated that data and information, no matter how important, that are not visible and readily accessible are soon ignored and forgotten. The same is true about the triad of organizational success factors. Consequently, the tremendous power of the "mother lode" of social institutions *rarely* gets the attention it rightly deserves.

One doesn't have to be a Noble Prize winner to be able to determine the reasons why these forces are commonly disregarded. Clearly, the most apparent cause for the gross oversight is the indiscernible and immeasurable characteristic of the triad. For instance, how do you quantify the levels of self-organization, social capital, and tacit knowledge of an enterprise? What amounts of these features are necessary to reassure success? How do you "manage" these resources? How do you account for them on financial statements?

Recall my example of the extremely high rate of business merger failures in Chapter Four. The main reason for the meager success rates was the inability of the parties involved to gauge the affects of the countless severed social relationships caused by a merger. That is, there was no entry for social capital and tacit knowledge on the financial reports used for the pre-merger analysis.

As a result, only the numbers of patents, copyrights, and unique operating processes on the ledgers could be used to measure the value of the intellectual assets of the firms involved. The informal social networks that produced the *explicit* knowledge never received any consideration at all in the deliberations. Hence, at least half of the value of each party's assets was unaccounted for.

Not only is the triad indiscernible it is also extremely dynamic. Therefore, how do you handle such a "hot potato?" You can't manage it in the traditional sense. Rather, it demands unmanagement. Naturally, in a controlled-access or hierarchical system, management's edict is to rigorously *control* organizational assets in order to assure that all resources (human and otherwise) are accounted for and productively applied.

That is well and good, but how do you deal with an elusive resource that's composed of autonomous voluntarily interconnected elements, held together by a strong common identity, and that never stops recreating itself? Worse, as soon as one tries to control the "thing," it reconfigures itself like an amoeba or breaks up and disappears.

Conventional management philosophy and its accompanying accounting standards effectively supporter the belief that if something can't be measured and controlled it probably isn't worthy of consideration. Put another way, if it's not something tangible it generally can't be included in financial statements (with the exception of goodwill—however it's defined) and, therefore, thought to provide little appreciable value to an organization. Ignorance is bliss.

Fortunately, there is hope that the accounting field is beginning to experiment with ways to measure intangible assets such as knowledge, relationships, emotions, and time.[3] What is regrettable is that the researchers are still trying to apply these new measures to controlled-access frameworks no matter how "flat" they may be. Mixing Knowledge Age accounting standards with Industrial Age structures will not produce the desired results. Does it really make sense having "knowledge managers" supervising knowledge workers? I don't think so.

Whether we like to admit it or not, hierarchical systems are *artificial* frameworks whose actions and activities are much less integrated than those of natural biological entities.[4] The reason for that should be relatively understandable by now. Hierarchical systems, founded on machine principles, are designed to facilitate the control of large assemblages of people by intimidation instead of attraction. These structures are not intended to allow individuals and small groups to self-organize, even though human nature can't be circumvented.

Consequently, controlled-access institutions by design are not geared to fully tap into the power of the triad of invisible organizational success factors. Recollect, that in hierarchies some individuals can perform at 20 to 30 percent of their ability without losing their jobs and that the average employee works only at two-thirds of his or her capacity. It never ceases to amaze me how much is accomplished in our enterprises daily, despite such an enormous misuse of our human potential. In any case, I am thoroughly convinced that by learning how to leverage the invisible wealth we can increase people's use of their potential abilities in our organizations to at least 80 percent. That, however, requires a biological rather than mechanistic perspective.

2.   ACTUATING THE HIDDEN TRIAD

It's now time to integrate all the suppositions, facts and figures presented in the previous chapters into a coherent whole representing the shared-access system and its interdependent components. I know of no other comprehensive framework, other than the shared-access arrangement, that is specifically designed to *support* the actuation of the hidden triad of organizational success factors. Hence, it also serves as a macro template for the general configurations of Knowledge Age organizations. Figure 8-1 depicts a shared-access system and its associated *dynamics elements* in its entirety.

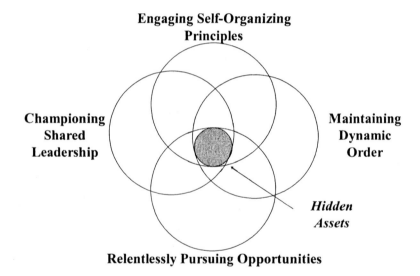

Figure 8-1. Shared-Access System Dynamics

Not a prescriptive system. What I've developed is not a prescriptive system where one size fits all because that is an impossible task when dealing with social entities. Every organization is unique in its make-up and operation. Rather, what I have created is a general integrated framework founded on proven principles incorporated from the latest findings in multiple disciplines. The principles I've delineated and integrated are grounded in common sense and practicality.

Further, what must also be understood is that I'm not in any way advocating genetic determinism. Rather, I am relying on the latest scientific research which clearly shows that our behavior is *genetically influenced* (not determined) and that we do have free will. Finally, the self-organizing principles that I am advocating are not only founded on the latest evolutionary research (such as anthropology, molecular biology, evolutionary biology, paleontology, etc.), but are also supported by the newest findings involving the self-organization of small groups and the basic tenets of chaos and complexity theories.

Dynamic focus. As portrayed by Figure 8-1, the dynamic focus of a shared-access system is deliberately on the actuation of the three interconnected organizational success factors or *invisible wealth*. Therefore, all the elements of the system must be wholly developed and running before the power of the triad is notably activated and experienced.

The results of the dynamic interchange of the four components of a shared-access entity are similar to the ingenious improvisations that emerge from the interplay (circular causality) of highly talented musicians in a first-rate jazz band. There is a common theme (vision) but there is no score to be followed because the group is an organic self-organizing system.

Serendipitously, each member takes turns leading the band (shared leadership) depending on the evolving melody (situation) and their interactions with the audience (environment). There is no limit to the ingenuity of the improvisations that the band can attain as they improve their abilities (core competencies) by constant practice. Thus, the music that surfaces from these emerging properties (social capital and tacit knowledge) is not only powerful and distinctive, but also impossible to replicate. Unfortunately for the linear thinkers among us, the energy emanating from the interplay of these dynamic forces can't be controlled or precisely measured.

Need for systems thinking. In order to fully comprehend the synergistic and symbiotic properties of living entities we need to start looking at ourselves and our social systems in terms of "wholes" and less in terms of "parts or components." That is, we need to rely more on systems or process thinking, since the biological world around us is composed of very dynamic and interdependent arrangement, not static structures.

Therefore, before taking a closer look at the elements of Figure 8-1 we need to again briefly recap the key differences between controlled- and shared-access systems. The major dissimilarity is that controlled-access institutions have static structures, whereas shared-access entities have form without structure. It is a subtle but an extremely important difference between the two systems.

A simple example for visualizing the distinction is a comparison between a clock and an amoeba. A clock consists of precise interchangeable parts assembled in accordance with predetermined blueprints. If it is not built correctly it will not keep time. If it malfunctions or a component wears out it stops running. Hence, a clock has an invariable structure and it can't repair itself without external intervention. An amoeba, on the other hand, has form but lacks a structure. That is, it is definitely an independent entity (it has form) but is not exactly identical to other amoebas, it can repair itself, and it constantly changes its shape in response to altering conditions.

Let's take it a step further. All self-organizing systems have form without structure to one degree or another. Every one of us, for instance, is an excellent example of this phenomenon. First, none of us is exactly identical physiologically. Our 30,000 to 40,000 genes work together in a self-organizing manner to help develop billions of neurons and trillions of cells in order to form a human being. Once formed, our bodies (including our bones) are in a constant state of flux maintaining dynamic order in response to internal and external conditions.

We have form without structure because mentally and physically we seldom, if ever, reach our outermost limits. Thus, we have an almost infinite capacity to grow and learn. For example, every part of our bodies is constantly being rejuvenated. We acquire a new liver every six to seven weeks and weakened parts of our brains get rebuilt through a process called neurogenesis. Most of us, even professional athletes, rarely fully exhaust our body's strength and endurance.

The same applies to our mental capacities. Yes, we all have dissimilar personalities and genetic predispositions (a center of gravity) but we rarely have an occasion to reach those unique individual outer limits. Accordingly, "the emphasis for research has largely shifted from structure to form— scientists now regard the brain not as a shell but as an active, dynamic, superbly plastic structure that changes from moment to moment."[5] We truly have form without structure.

The shared-access system. Looking at Figure 8-1 we can see that the four self-organizing principles discussed in Chapter Five are the catalyst or the starting point for the shared-access system. Without individual autonomy, a shared identity, challenging aspirations and dynamic alignment, widespread *open* (as opposed to underground) self-organization would be curtailed since most people's innate drives wouldn't be expressed in a balanced manner. As a result, the development of social capital would be restricted and with it the voluntary sharing of tacit knowledge.

Further, an institution lacking open self-organization would have great difficulty in championing shared leadership. That is, budding leaders need a supportive organizational context and a meaningful common vision in order to emerge. They need to broaden their talents by being encouraged to wrap their arms around more complex problems and opportunities in concert with other more seasoned committed associates.

A shared-access system also needs requisite variety in order to properly respond to fluid wide-reaching conditions. In order to accomplish that, clan members have to be able to differentiate between the complementary properties of tacit and explicit knowledge. In essence, associates shouldn't lose sight of the fact that unconnected know-how is the wellspring of all new knowledge which provides additional requisite variety. Additionally, the overall relentless pursuit of opportunities needs to be centered on the organization's evolving (as opposed to static) core competencies. Finally, overlapping feedback and feedforward schemes (discussed in the last chapter) provide an organization dynamic order by supporting environmental scanning, forecasting, development of higher awareness, and a clear picture of ongoing activities.

As one can see, without the activation of all four interdependent elements displayed by Figure 8-1 the hidden dynamic forces of a venture will remain, by and large, untapped. Hence, organizational success is primarily dependent on how much continuous attention its invisible wealth receives. For that reason it warrants a closer look.

Hidden assets. It's important for two reasons to clearly differentiate between the four elements of a shared-access system and its core, hidden assets, "brought to life" by the interactive elements. First, the dynamics of both the larger system and its subsystem are barely discernible and not easily quantifiable, at least not through conventional means. Second, before anyone decides to put an intangible framework to practical use they need to understand it in considerable detail. The application of quantum physics is a fitting example of phenomena that is undetectable by the naked eye but valid and usable nevertheless.

Fundamentally, a shared-access system provides the dynamic environmental context that fuels the actuation of the generally dormant interactive triad of organizational success factors. Thus, the hidden assets or invisible wealth of an institution is a relatively self-contained subsystem and social resource that is stirred into action by the noninvasive support (unmanagement) of a shared-access setting.

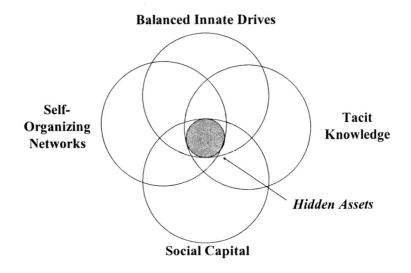

Figure 8-2. Hidden Assets

Figure 8-2 is a detailed representation of organizational hidden assets or the "mother lode." Note that it is composed of the triad of organizational success factors in addition to the balanced expression of human innate drives. The balanced activation of people's genetic predispositions serves as a catalyst for the *organization-wide* (as opposed to scattered pockets dispersed around an enterprise) actuation of the three interactive forces comprising the mother lode. However, as one can see, a shared-access system must first be in place in order to support the balanced expression of people's innate drives.

Clearly, the overall process is very fluid where one system continuously sustains the other. For instance, extensive institution-wide overt self-organizing (as contrasted with clandestine localized occurrences) will begin to develop only when there is a social context in place that fosters the balanced expression of people's innate drives. Once that is set in motion more and more voluntary collaborative connections develop throughout an organization which leads to the generation of higher levels of social capital. Concurrently, increased levels of tacit knowledge emerge and are shared among clan members, facilitating innovation and the expansion of requisite variety.

3. KEY MAINTENANCE PROCESSES

In a shared-access system every member of the clan is responsible and accountable for the success of the venture. There are no "bosses" to give commands, define goals, and tell people how to carry out their commitments. Accordingly, there are certain key processes that need to be constantly maintained and reinforced for the overt self-organizing system to function properly. I will briefly highlight five of these practices.

Shared leadership and commitment. Every member of a shared-access system should be prepared and willing to assume a leadership role depending on the problem or opportunity confronted by the institution. There are no exceptions if an individual truly wants to be a member of the system. Leadership in the clan is based on talent, skills and experience, not on position power. Consequently, every associate needs to be ready to take the lead whenever his or her expertise warrants and others are prepared to follow without giving up their individual autonomy.

It must also be remembered that in a shared-access organization everyone makes their own commitments and is expected to fulfill them. Moreover, if a member discovers an opportunity that looks promising or a problem that needs attention, they should bring those matters to the attention of other members immediately. In addition, they need to initiate action to resolve the issue either on their own or by persuading others to join them in the undertaking. Of course, each member must also be prepared to join others whenever that seems most appropriate. It is vital that everybody in the clan be proactive.

Shared-access associates should constantly be asking the following or similar questions of themselves:

- How well have I identified my talents, skills, and experiences to the rest of the clan?
- How well do I know the talents, skills, and backgrounds of my colleagues?
- How proactive am I in looking for problems and opportunities that would enhance the activities of the entire organization?
- When was the last time I spoke to one of our customers, suppliers, or external network members?
- How often do I read journals or books and browse a variety of databases (both within and outside my field of expertise) and share what I have learned with my associates?

- When was the last time I volunteered to lead a project?
- How many projects or tasks have I made commitments to? Am I over extended? How far am I willing to stretch myself?
- How willing am I to mentor others with less experience?

As one can see, the emphasis in a shared-access system is on generating as many voluntary connections as possible, which naturally starts at the individual level. Again, being proactive is critical for sustaining the above process. That, however, doesn't suggest that everyone in the clan needs to be a "social animal."

We are all geared to collaborate with one another as long as we see a benefit to both the overall organization and ourselves. In the right social context, people can be assertive without forcing others to resort to either innate fight (aggressive) or flight (submissive) tendencies. Being assertive "means protecting one's space, time, and integrity by allowing others to influence outcomes without taking advantage of or abusing others."[6]

Unadulterated teamwork. Autonomous teams accomplish much of the work in an overt self-organizing system. That definitely doesn't mean that individual effort is not valued. It certainly is. In fact, real teams are composed of well talented, independently minded individuals who are also *willing* to work with others because they know the value of voluntary collaboration. Teamwork is all about synergy or realizing what can be accomplished more creatively, better, and faster through interdependent efforts.

Fundamentally, in a shared-access system teams are comprised of volunteers, are well skilled technically and in group processes, and obviously govern themselves. Individuals can also be members of more than one team. Further, because they are very autonomous, teams must be keenly aware of what all other teams are doing in order to avoid sub-optimizing their efforts to the detriment of the entire organization.

Close interdependent relationships (individually and in teams) allow institutional members to take advantage of the mutually beneficial growth that occurs when people interact voluntarily. In essence, in real teams all members feel a responsibility and desire towards one another to be both teacher and learner. That is to say, learning is most effective when we reveal what we think we know to the entire team and clan in order that it can then be examined, challenged, and improved upon before the idea(s) is put to use.

The following questions can be asked to determine if a team is functioning effectively:
- Is team membership completely voluntary?
- Is team training available on demand?
- Are all the team members familiar with organizational core competencies?

- Can all members clearly articulate the interdependence of their tasks and the specific goal(s) of the team?
- Is the team convinced that their self-imposed goals stretch their capabilities?
- Have definite timelines been agreed upon for the accomplishment of goals and is everyone in the clan able to track those timelines?
- Are interrelationships with other teams clearly defined and monitored?
- Do members encourage one another to detect problems/opportunities and to share those discoveries?
- Are differences as to what everyone needs to contribute to the team openly discussed?
- Is experimentation encouraged within the team?
- Is there high interest to learn from other teams and individuals?

Perpetuating shared identity. Clearly, for overt self-organization to function properly it must depend on more than cooperative associates and teams. Therefore, it is also important that the clan develops and maintains a strong sense of shared identity and community. A community is a place where people feel free to share their deepest thoughts with one another because they believe that they have a common destiny. It is a place where members truly believe that they belong and where compassion and empathy are the basis for most relationships. Thus, it is an environment where human innate drives have the best opportunity to be expressed in a balanced manner.

A real community, with a strong awareness of a shared identity is more akin to a closely-knit extended family than a formal entity. It is a safe haven where unrestrained trust, reciprocity, and a sense of interdependence reign. A shared-access system functions more on jointly shared ambition than on publicly acknowledged policies and directives. Consequently, a strong sense of community and shared identity are the essence of social capital.

At the same time, such a community doesn't try to inhibit healthy disagreements among its members. On the contrary—it supports them enthusiastically. Healthy exchanges of differing perspectives, conducted in an atmosphere of trust and respect, are the very foundation of challenging mutually beneficial aspirations and a common vision.

Periodic answers to the following questions should provide a measure of the strength of a clan's shared identity and its level of social capital:
- Are informal groups and networks performing their activities and interactions more and more visibly?
- Are there any indications whether some of the self-organizing groups and networks are working clandestinely? If yes, what is causing that? (Divergent aspirations? Power struggles? Threats?)

- Are associates and teams encouraging free expression of diverse perspectives, values and beliefs?
- Are new ideas welcomed and enthusiastically explored?
- How unrestrained are the levels of trust, reciprocity, and interdependence?
- Is there a strong sense of belonging, compassion, and empathy among the members?
- Do most people feel responsible and accountable for both their actions and the performance of the clan as a whole?
- Do associates feel that rewards are distributed equitably?

Self-reference. Overt self-organization involving all institutional members, without individual self-reference founded on mutually beneficial challenging aspirations, is analogous to an attempt to "herd cats." Hence, for self-organization to succeed clan members need to develop a frame of reference that allows them, even when "alone in the desert," to act in a manner that is beneficial to both them and the enterprise.

Recall the explanation of life's common purpose in Chapter Three. What that suggests is that for an individual to develop a self-reference that also includes the welfare of the organization, he or she must be convinced that reciprocity is the best option for survival. Or, since a shared-access system is entirely dependent on voluntary cooperation that allows it to function without a formal structure, there has to be a way to keep its members headed in the same direction. A common vision is that instrument.

A true common vision is a living document that keeps clan members focused on mutually beneficial goals and objectives without undue formal restraints. Thus, considerable time and effort must be devoted to its development and maintenance. In fact, the process of putting the document together and getting total buy-in from everyone is as important as the final results. In this manner the common vision also imparts a strong notion of self-reference to everyone involved that acts like an internal compass that point in the right direction night and day.

Key questions that should be asked by clan members periodically:

- Are my personal survival needs best satisfied by being a member of this organization?
- What do we want to accomplish together?
- Who are we trying to serve?

Feedback and feedforward. Maintaining dynamic order based on real-time data and information is another vital process necessary for the operation of a shared-access system. After all, information is the lifeblood of all self-organizing entities. Without constant *deliberate* exchange of information, a wide-ranging overt self-organizing system has a good chance of fragmenting into smaller entities that may, unknowingly, develop objectives that deviate from the overall vision of the clan.

In order to prevent that from happening individuals and teams should make a conscious effort to carry out the following:

- Maintain a relatively thorough understanding of what all members and teams are doing and how their activities are related and impacted by those actions.
- Provide continuous up-to-date information on current and anticipated activities to all clan members.
- Regularly scan the environment for pertinent information and trends, and share the findings with others in the clan.
- Maintain close relations with customers, suppliers, and external organizational network members.
- Be proactive and try to anticipate the future.

As much as possible, the actions above should be accomplished on a face-to-face basis and backed up with very visible displays easily accessed by all members of the organization. Members and teams should also be able to track financial data and determine to what extent their activities are adding value to the enterprise. After all, equitable (as opposed to equal) compensation, as briefly explained in Chapter Seven, can only be accomplished through open book management. Again, systems thinking is indispensable on the part of everyone in a shared-access arrangement.

4. A HEALTHIER AND MORE PRODUCTIVE FUTURE

I believe we can now better visualize what physiological and psychological impact an individual may experience in either a controlled- or shared-access environment. In a clockwork or mechanistic organizational context, a person will probably experience considerable stress due to its confining and uncongenial climate. Worse, people will seldom get the opportunity to stretch their almost limitless wings, other than possibly clandestinely, leaving the triad of organizational success factors untapped. Private and public institutions that are able to only sway members to support the official goals with a scant twenty to sixty percent of their potential capacities can't be very healthy places to work in.

Clearly, a shared-access system is a much better option for many organizations than a controlled-access arrangement. Knowing that people are in a self-organizing mode 24 hours a day, seven days a week should convince us to rely more on that phenomenon than ignoring it or pushing it underground. More importantly, why not fully release the forces of the informal networks that accomplish most of the work in organizations to begin with? Organic systems that have form without structure not only enable people to grow and learn exponentially, but they are also much more productive.

Hence, it should be quite apparent by now why knowledge workers can't be managed in the traditional ways as advocated by Frederick Taylor at the dawn of the 20th century. As concluded by Richard Florida's research:

> ...creative work cannot be taylorized like rote work in the old factory or office, for several reasons. First, creative work is not repetitive. Second, because a lot of it goes on inside people's heads, you literally cannot see it happening—and you can't taylorize what you can't see. Finally, creative people tend to rebel at efforts to manage them overly systematically.[7]

Finally, people who are still a little unsettled about the viability of shared-access systems should focus their attention on the growing number of knowledge professionals in today's labor force. You can only "bribe" them with money up to a certain point and not beyond in order to attain their knowledge. What that means is that if you want to retain good knowledge workers and the know-how that goes with it, you must not only give them a "piece of the action" but also collective power. As Peter Drucker has stated:

> Increasingly, performance in these knowledge-based industries will come to depend on running the institution so as to attract, hold, and motivate knowledge workers. When this can no longer be done by satisfying knowledge workers' greed, as we are now trying to do, it will have to be done by satisfying their values, and by giving them social recognition and social power. It will have to be done by turning them from subordinates into fellow executives, and from employees, however well paid, into partners.[8]

In the final analysis today's organizations must thrive in a turbulent and constantly changing global environment where the generation of leading edge intellectual capital is the dominant success factor. Thus, enterprises that are perceived to be and are run like biological systems instead of clocks or machines will lead the pack. Their strategies will also be based on an ecological integrated network perspective[9] rather than looking at the world as a set of standalone market segments.

Conversely, organizations that fail to grasp the fundamental importance of human nature from an interconnected self-organizing point of view will wither like grapes on the vine in the long-run. Ignoring the invisible power of the dynamic interrelated triad of organizational success factors will undoubtedly lead to catastrophic results in the Knowledge Age.

EPILOGUE
Costly Neglect

In *every* social system tremendous levels of vigor and ingenuity are poised to emerge, needing only the proper organizational context to be fully activated. Regrettably, most administrators either ignore these hidden assets because they can't be controlled and "formally" accounted for or they are simply oblivious of the large dormant resources going to waste all around them. Worse, both types of managers are most likely working with an Industrial Age mind-set, trying their best to keep refining the hierarchy and wondering why they're having little success.

Without knowing how tap into the "invisible wealth" of our organizations, we will continue to allow 80 percent of mergers to fail to achieve their projected benefits; scratch our heads as most change efforts fall short of their targets; grimace when some individuals only perform at 20 to 30 percent of their ability; and knowingly expect the average employee to work merely at two-thirds of his or her capacity. That truly is a costly neglect of human nature and potential.

In order to fully unleash the hidden power and wealth of the "real" organizational success factors, an institution must shift its overall framework from a hierarchy (flat or tall) to an open self-organizing system. Thus, the new system should, like an amoeba, have form without a rigid structure and attain cooperation of its activities voluntarily without all sorts of supervision and control mechanisms. It's not an easy process, but one can only imagine the long-run benefits a venture can achieve striving for that goal.

I have illustrated how four invisible yet potent organizational features account for nearly two thirds of the potential of a firm. Being mindful of the genetic behavioral influences we're all endowed with, each in his/her unique way is the starting point. Essentially, human nature is the catalyst that sets the invisible triad of organizational success factors into motion, leading to increased overall institutional innovation and wealth.

Further, these success factors work best in a dynamic and integrated fashion. That is, without widely and openly practiced self-organization (voluntary interactions and networks) an enterprise will be unable to develop high levels of social capital (trusting and reciprocal relationships). Without adequate social capital, people will not see the need to share new ideas (tacit knowledge) and the organization will degenerate from lack of innovation.

Depending on the structure of an enterprise (a hierarchy or an amoeba—controlled-access or shared-access), the outcomes of the dynamic interactions of the triad can be positive, neutral or negative. That is, if the member's innate drives can be expressed in a relatively balanced fashion, then the informal systems should be relatively supportive of the organizational activities.

If not, the emergent networks will most likely be pushed underground, lessening the development of social capital and the sharing of tacit knowledge. Hence, the actions of the informal networks may not affect the formal system at all (they are neutral and primarily for amusement) or if the organization's quality of life is quite poor, they may, to one degree or another, even deliberately undercut the desired goals of a given venture.

1.   THINGS TO KEEP IN MIND

For an organization to be able to tap into its hidden assets, it needs to start moving from a hierarchical configuration to an increasingly voluntary collaborative arrangement. This means leaving a compliance oriented work context behind and replacing it with one where commitment is the dominant interactive force. In order to accomplish that feat, the following guiding principles should be adhered to:

- Select the right people
- Practice "positive" individual autonomy
- Develop a shared identity
- Embrace challenging aspirations
- Practice dynamic alignment

Select the right people. Who you invite to join your venture will help you or break you. First, you are literally searching for "new family members" or partners, not just for employees who can perform certain tasks. In essence, you want to assure that both sides of human nature have a chance to be expressed by all organizational members. That can only take place among close friends. "Employees" are mercenaries who normally run to the highest bidders. Partners or real associates, on the other hand, are part owners whose welfare depends on the present and future success of an organization.

Second, you want people who have a long-term interest in your organization. Retention of members is vital. Without wide-ranging relationships and close cooperation, which take considerable time to evolve, high levels of social capital are impossible to develop and maintain. Third, you want to find people who have certain talents that would have a major positive impact on the success of a company. Talents are similar to innate drives in that they are genetically based. If that was not the case, everybody could become a great painter, test pilot or super athlete.

Finally, you need to invite people to join the firm who are self-reliant, highly motivated, and conscientious. At the same time, they should be willing to work alone or in teams. They should also be ready to take full responsibility and accountability for the successes and failures of the organization as a whole. You expect that from partners.

Practice "positive" individual autonomy. People need to understand that a partnership demands that each affiliate contributes something valuable to a venture. A self-organizing system functions on the synergy of its combined resources, hard work, and perseverance of the people involved. There are no entitlements, only rewards and satisfaction from results achieved.

This means that people must know what their abilities and proficiencies are and, above all, how to effectively apply them on their own or in concert with other people. After all, the underpinnings of the power of the invisible triad reside in the combined talents and efforts applied *willingly* by its members. In addition, in a self-organizing system individual autonomy is counter balanced by the necessity that members also be highly socially responsible and accountable. They everyone should be willing to collaborate with others.

In such steadfast voluntary relationships, all parties concerned are very dependent on two interrelated qualities—interdependence and reciprocity. Self-reliant individuals learn that autonomy needs to be tempered with interdependence. Thus, helping others to grow also has a positive impact on the mentor. Moreover, that means being the enabler in one case and willingness to become the apprentice in another as conditions warrant.

Furthermore, valid partnerships are dependent on reciprocity. This, of course, suggests that ideas and other resources are readily shared for mutual benefits. As importantly, all members should also be ready and able to assume both leadership and follower roles as conditions change. Leadership in a self-organizing system has absolutely nothing to do with "position power" or with "bossing" people around but instead is based on expertise and the willingness to distribute that know-how widely. Therefore, as the need for a particular expertise or talent changes from one problem or opportunity to the next, so does the acceptance and assumption of leadership.

Develop a shared identity. Every close-knit social entity has a very unique shared identity or special chemistry that, like glue, holds it together through good times and bad. Like a clan, it is a distinctive living and breathing biological system with its own needs and goals as it tries to survive as best as possible in its particular environment. This shared identity is unique for two reasons. First, each group is made up of distinctive members. That alone makes each social body different from another.

Second, after a group is formed, it begins to develop unique voluntary connections between its constituents as the members seek to pursue their perceived survival options (self-organize) within the assemblage. Clearly, the more open this process is and remains, the more constructive and group specific these networks become. Also, over time these associations become more supportive and intense. Consequently, the unique set of people and the connections that evolve between them produces the shared identity within a clan that only they can put to productive use. Just as importantly, that uniqueness can't be emulated by another social entity, no matter how they might try. That gives an organization a definite competitive advantage.

Moreover, we need to keep in mind that most people are incapable of establishing relatively close ties with more than about 150 people. Thus, a self-organizing mode of operation is only effective with groups of 150 or less members. In larger clusters relationships become fragmented, ties of common interest cannot be effectively maintained, and hierarchies creep in. In effect, within more sizable groups overall close social ties weaken or disappear, becoming confined to small separate cliques, and various formalized "control" systems slowly begin to take shape.

Small size alone, however, will fall short of facilitating the emergence of a truly evocative shared identity. One of the most effective ways of developing unrestrained trust and a sense of interdependence among people, and increasing the robustness of the shared identity within an organization is through autonomous self-managing teams.

Embrace challenging aspirations. Challenging aspirations provide an organization an internal compass that helps to keep all its members and teams advancing towards common objectives without the necessity for conventional policies, directives and supervision. Goals must give organizational affiliates much more than direction. They not only have to be challenging but also inspiring.

Hence, in a self-organizing system, defining challenging and aspiring goals is a never-ending dynamic process, involving all associates where the focus is on both self-interest and mutual benefits. The outcome of this continuous interdependent process is a *living document* called the common vision. Consequently, the process of putting the common vision together and getting total buy-in from all group members is at least as essential as the final product, which in reality never is completely finalized.

Practice dynamic alignment. In a self-organizing environment there are no bosses who make all the decisions and issuing every orders. Rather, every member of the organization must be ready and willing to take the helm when a fitting moment presents itself. They must also be willing to follow when that is the best option. Accordingly, dynamic alignment is all about shared or situational leadership, consensus decision-making, systems thinking, and individual commitment. That is precisely one of the main reasons for the vigorous selection process.

2.   SOME CLOSING THOUGHTS

Life is a balancing act. Our minds and bodies are in constant search for dynamic order as we seek to fulfill life's common purpose—living long enough to successfully perpetuate the species—with every action we take within our immediate surroundings.

Unsurprisingly, the search for dynamic order also occurs in our places of work as each of us seeks to make our daily bread. Therefore, doesn't it make good sense to deliberately design our social institutions to support people's "natural" efforts in pursuing their life's common purpose, instead of having them waste considerable time and energy in half-heartedly supporting or even hindering official policies and goals? I believe smart enterprises will learn how to leverage the power of the invisible trial of organizational success factors in the future. They will grasp the wisdom of individual and organizational balance.

We have a four billion year history that we should be more aware and appreciative of. I certainly am not ashamed of the fact that I am in some manner related to every living organism on our planet. In fact, I take great joy in knowing I have more relatives than I will ever have the occasion to meet personally. It is also gratifying for me to know that even tiny zebrafish have some genes that are identical to humans and are now being used for human genetic research.1 Isn't it high time that we take what science has already provided us and apply it to the human side of our organizations and our lives in general?

It's to our advantage to know that we still have imprinted in our genes the innate predispositions to be both the most violent as well as the most egalitarian creatures in the world. Hence, we *can* learn how to develop social institutions that minimize hostility and maximize voluntary interdependent activities. We innately prefer to live in small egalitarian groups. So, why do we keep ignoring that fact in most of our social institutions?

Clearly, there is now sufficient scientific evidence, especially in molecular biology and the neurosciences, for us to set old myths aside and begin to admit who we really are. Just acknowledging that humans function best in environments where biological principles are adhered to rather than in contexts governed by mechanistic rules and regulations would be a tremendous leap forward.

We could start by looking at ourselves and our social systems in terms of "wholes" and less in terms of "parts or components." That is, we need to rely more on systems or process thinking since the biological world around us is mostly composed of very interdependent dynamic activities and not static structures. It is also time to fill the gap between management concepts based on the "visible" organizational elements such as structure, rewards, strategy, et cetera and the assortment of motivational theories requiring leaders to have a deep psychological awareness of each individual in order to motivate them to their best effort.

Humans function best in an environment where they are able to express both categories of their innate drives in a balanced manner. Thus, people need to be able to take care of both their personal needs and at the same time *believe that cooperating with others provides significant mutual benefits.* In essence, our genetic predispositions are the catalytic forces that influence how informal networks form and function within social groups.

Unwittingly, most of today's organizations with their customary hierarchical management structures are mainly impacting their people's self-centered drives as they pursue their best perceived *individual* survival options. Simultaneously, their leaders are asking these individuals to be good team players and deeply committed to the goals of the enterprise. Clearly, this is not the most effective way to run an enterprise and expect the informal networks to fully support its official goals and objectives.

We are born with the capacity to anticipate and to respond to changes in our immediate environment in addition to learning from our experiences. So, whether we like to admit it or not, all activities and interactions between people are governed by the principles of self-organization. Consequently, we need to learn what some of the essential principles of self-organization are in order to draw on the power of emergent social systems.

Without understanding how to take advantage of the limitless potential of invisible wealth, an enterprise will curb its capabilities in the years to come. That's a tremendous waste of vast quantities of unrevealed human knowledge and energy. It's also the primary difference between institutional success and failure. *We should keep in mind that life by and large is good when one pursues things that are good for life in general!*

APPENDIX A
Data Systems International Vision

OUR VISION

Common Purpose
To help organizations become more successful by providing people unlimited collaboration capabilities.

Core Values
We will maintain high-sustained levels of our core values, with everyone taking complete responsibility and accountability for the success of each endeavor and the company as a whole.

- Integrity
- Adhere to high moral values.
- Practice intellectual honesty.
- See all situations as they really are and not as you wish them to be.
- Trust.
- Rely on the character, ability, strength, and conviction of our associates.
- All our interactions (with each other, our customers, vendors, partners and external networks) are based on honesty, trust, compassion and commitment.
- We keep all our commitments.
- Shared Leadership.
- Everyone is capable and willing to take the lead or follow, depending on the situation.
- Leadership is based on expertise and preparedness; not on position power.
- Urgency, persistence, buy-in, teaching, and coaching are all part of the process.
- Make commitments and produce results to the commitment.

- Embrace continual change.
- Teamwork.
- Promote self-direction, interdependence, mutuality, and reciprocity.
- Champion collaboration with internal and external networks.
- Share and build on each other's knowledge.
- Innovation
- Demonstrate an uncanny ability to continuously enhance our core competencies in order to create new or modified products and services.
- Provide the highest value at the lowest cost for our clients.
- Strive persistently to do the impossible.

Whom are we trying to serve?

We will help any organization, including ours, interested in finding innovative ways to better serve our clients.

What do we want to accomplish together?

Our vision is to make organizations successful worldwide by developing and providing innovative products and services.

We will accomplish this by nurturing a collaborative learning environment and continually improving our core competencies, productivity, products, services, and overall effectiveness.

We will strive to be one of the world's most innovative and sought-after companies and, in the process, have as much fun as possible.

Our Long-Range Goal

Our long-range goal is to become a *well-respected and profitable* $350 million Application Service Provider (ASP) business by the year 2010. We will know that we've reached our goal when we hit the monetary target and also have attained the following status:

- We are respected and admired by other ASP organizations and our competitors.
- Our innovative solutions are actively sought out around the world.
- We have pride in ourselves and the best people will constantly seek to join our team.
- Both our associates and customers will know that our organization has contributed to their lives in a very positive way.

APPENDIX B
Sample Team Activity Tracking Display

Team XYZ Tasks
Projects:
- Lead for developing a Heated Portable Stadium Seat.
- Supporting Team A, B, and H projects.

Initial Plan A:

January	February	March	April	May	June
Requirements	Design	Build	Test	Market	Production
	Prototype	Test	Test	Test	Service
Adjusted Forecast:					
	May	Aug.	Oct.	Jan Yr. B	Mar. Yr. B
Actual:					
	May	Aug.	Oct.		

Other Teams Involved:
- Team P
- Team M
- Team L

Problems or Opportunities:
- Problem — Design and placement of heating coils consumed extra time.
- Opportunity — Design and attach small easily accessible plastic enclosure /poncho to the seat. Will produce 2 types of seats: one without and one with a cover. Forecasted full production and delivery dates shouldn't be affected.

Individual External Assignments:
- Hollie—Checking the capabilities of 3 parts suppliers.

- Matt— Coordinating marketing and distribution options with 2 selected firms.
- Ryan—Looking for manufacturing joint ventures in Europe and Far East.
- Sarah—Working with a consumer products testing company.

NOTES

INTRODUCTION

1. Kelso, J.A.S. (1995) Dynamic Patterns: The Self-Organization of Brain and Behavior. Bradford Books, MIT Press, Cambridge, MA.
   Stevens, A. and Price, T. (1996) Evolutionary Psychiatry: A New Beginning. Routledge, New York, NY.
2. Roethlisberger, F.J. and Dickson, W.J. (1939) Management and the Worker. Harvard University Press, Cambridge, MA.
3. Cross, R. and Prusak, L. (2002) "The People Who Make Organizations Go—or Stop," Harvard Business Review, June 2002, pp. 105-112.
   Lengnick-Hall, M.L. and Lengnick-Hall, C.A. (2003) "HR's Role in Building Relationship Networks," Academy of Management Executive, Vol. 17, No. 4, pp. 54-63.
   Shirky, C. (2004) "Watching the Patterns Emerge" in "Breakthrough Ideas for 2004." Harvard Business Review, February, pp. 13-37.
4. Watts, D. J. (2003) Six Degrees. W. W. Norton & Company, Inc., New York, NY.
5. Ehin, C. (2000) Unleashing Intellectual Capital, Butterworth-Heinemann, Boston, MA.
6. Morris, H.J. (2001) "Happiness Explained," U.S. News & World Report, September 3.
7. Monastersky, R. (1998) "The Rise of Life on Earth," National Geographic, March.
   Stevens, A. and Price, T. (1996) Evolutionary Psychiatry: A New Beginning. Routledge, New York, NY.
8. Restak, R. (1984) The Brain. Bantam Books, New York, NY.
9. Barash, D.P. and Barash, I.L. (2000) The Mammal in the Mirror. W.H. Freeman and Company, New York, NY.
10. Pinker, S. (2002) The Blank Slate: The Modern Denial of Human Nature. Viking Penguin, New York, NY.

CHAPTER 2

1. Florida, R. (2004) "No Monopoly on Creativity" in "Breakthrough Ideas for 2004," Harvard Business Review, February, pp. 13-37.
2. Cohen, W.M. and Levinthal, D.A. (1990) "A New Perspective on   Learning and Innovation," *Administrative Science Quarterly,* Vol. 35, pp. 128-152.
3. Zahra, S.A. and George, G. (2002) "Absorptive Capacity: A Review, Reconceptualization, and Extension," *The Academy of Management   Review,* April, Vol. 27 (2), pp. 185-203.
4. Zahra, S.A. and George, G. (2002) "Absorptive Capacity: A Review, Reconceptualization, and Extension," *The Academy of Management   Review,* April, Vol. 27 (2), pp. 185-203.
5. Smith, L. (2001) "The Concept of Intellectual Capital in Mergers and   Acquisitions," Unpublished MBA research paper at Westminster   College of Salt Lake City, UT., Spring.
6. Scanlan, B.K. (1981)"Creating a Climate for Achievement," *Business   Horizons,* Mach-April, pp. 5-9.
7. Polanyi, M. (1958) *Personal Knowledge: Towards a Post-Critical   Philosophy.* University of Chicago Press, Chicago, IL.
   Stewart, T.A. (1997) *Intellectual Capital: The New Wealth of Organizations.* Doubleday/Currency, New York, NY.
   Sveiby, K.E. (1997) *The New Organizational Wealth: Managing &Measuring Knowledge-Based Assets.* Berrett-Koehler, San Francisco, CA.
8. Le Doux, J. (2002) *Synaptic Self: How Our Brains Become Who We Are.*   Penguin Books, New York, NY.
9. Morris, H.J. (2001) "Happiness Explained," *U.S. News & World Report,*   September 3, pp. 46-54.
10. Barash, D.P. and Barash, I.L. (2000) *The Mammal in the Mirror.* W.H.   Freeman and Company, New York, NY.
11. "Future Visions," (2003) *Time,* February 17, pp. 60-61.
12. Bakan, D. (1966) *The Duality of Human Existence.* Beacon Books,   Boston, MA.
    Chance, M.R.A. (1988) "Introduction," in *Social Fabrics of the Mind* edited by M.R.A. Chance. Lawrence Erlbaum, Hove and London, Hillsdale, NJ.
    Stevens, A. and Price, T. (1996) *Evolutionary Psychiatry: A New   Beginning.* Routledge, New York, NY.
13. Dunbar, R. (1996) *Grooming, Gossip, and the Evaluation of Language.* Harvard University Press, Cambridge, MA.
    Nicholson, N. (1997) "Evolutionary Psychology: Toward a New View of   Human Nature and Organizational Society," *Human Relations,* Vol.50,   No. 9, pp. 1053-1078.
14. Sagan, C. (1977) *The Dragons of Eden.* Random House, New York, NY.

CHAPTER 3

1. Barash, D.P. and Barash, I.L. (2000) *The Mammal in the Mirror.* W.H. Freeman and Company, New York, NY.

   Restak, R. (1984) *The Brain.* Bantam Books, New York, NY

2. Pinker, S. (2002) *The Blank Slate: The Modern Denial of Human Nature.* Viking Penguin, New York, NY.

3. Stevens, A. and Price, T. (1996) *.Evolutionary Psychiatry: A New Beginning.* Routledge, New York, NY.

4. Wilson, E.O. (1998) *Consilience: The Unity of Knowledge.* Knopf, New York, NY.

5. Pinker, S. (2002) The Blank Slate: The Modern Denial of Human Nature. Viking Penguin, New York, NY.

6. Gould, S.J. (1993) *Eight Little Piggies: Reflections in Natural History.* Norton, New York, NY.

   Raup, D.M. (1991) *Extinction: Bad Genes or Bad Luck?* Norton, New York, NY.

7. Eldredge, N. and Gould, S.J. (1972) "Punctuated Equilibria: An Alternative to Phyletic Gradualism." In *Models of Paleobiology,* edited by T.J.M. Schopf, pp. 82-115. Freeman, Cooper and Co., San Francisco, CA.

8. Mayer, E. (2001) *What Evolution Is.* Basic Books, New York, NY.

9. Pasternak, C. A. (2003) Quest: The Essence of Humanity. John Wiley & Sons Ltd., West Sussex, England.

10. MacLean, P.D. (1973) *A Triune Concept of the Brain Behavior.* University of Toronto Press, Toronto, Canada.

    Stevens, A. and Price, T. (1996) *.Evolutionary Psychiatry: A New Beginning.* Routledge, New York, NY.

    Williams, G. (1966) *Adaption and Natural Selection.* Princeton University Press, Princeton, NJ.

11. Power, M. (1991) *The Egalitarians—Human and Chimpanzee.* Cambridge University Press, New York, NY.

12. Diamond, J. (1992) *The Third Chimpanzee.* Harper Collins Publishers, New York, NY.

    Gore, R. (1997) "Tracking the First of Our Kind," *National Geographic,* Vol. 192, No. 3, pp. 92-99.

    Gore, R. (1997) "The Dawn of Humans," *National Geographic,* Vol. 192, No. 1, pp. 96-113.

    Linden, E. (1992) "A Curious Kinship: Apes and Humans," *National Geographic,* Vol. 189, No. 1, pp. 2-45.

    Leakey, R. and Lewin, R. (1992) *Origins Reconsidered: In Search of What Makes Us Human.* Doubleday, New York, NY.

    Ridley, M. (1999) *Genome.* Harper Collins Publishers, New York, NY.

13. Lee, R.B. (1979) *The !Kung San: Men, Women and Work in a Foraging Society.* Cambridge University Press, London, England.

Marshall, L. (1976) *The !Kung of Nyae Nyae.* Harvard University Press, Cambridge, MA.

Power, M. (1991) *The Egalitarians—Human and Chimpanzee.* Cambridge University Press, New York, NY.

Yellen, J.E. (1990) "The Transformation of the Kalahari Kung," *Scientific   American,* April, pp. 99-105.

14. Mayer, E. (2001) *What Evolution Is.* Basic Books, New York, NY.

15. Ehin, C. (1995) "The Quest for Empowering Organizations: Some Lessons From Our Foraging Past," *Organization Science,* November-December, pp. 666-671.

Harris, M. (1989) "Life Without Chiefs," *New Age Journal,* November-   December, pp. 42-45.

16. Dunbar, R. (1996) *Grooming, Gossip, and the Evaluation of Language.* Harvard University Press, Cambridge, MA.

17. Allman, J.M. (1999) *Evolving Brains.* Scientific American Library, New   York, NY.

Dunbar, R. (1996) *Grooming, Gossip, and the Evaluation of Language*   Harvard University Press, Cambridge, MA.

Zimmer, C. (2003) "Great Mysteries of Human Evolution," *Discover,* September,   pp. 33-43.

18. Stanford, C. (2001) *Significant Others: The Ape-Human Continuum and   the Quest for Human Nature.* Basic Books, New York, NY.

19. Hallowell, E.M. (1999) "The Human Moment at Work," *Harvard   Business Review,* January-February, pp. 58-66.

20. Morris, H.J. (2001) "Happiness Explained," *U.S. News & World Report,*   September 3, pp. 46-54.

21. Bakan, D. (1966) *The Duality of Human Existence.* Beacon Books,   Boston, MA.

Chance, M.R.A. (1988) "Introduction," in *Social Fabrics of the Mind,* edited by M.R.A. Chance. Lawrence Erlbaum, Hove and London, Hillsdale, NJ.

Stevens, A. and Price, T. (1996) *Evolutionary Psychiatry: A New Beginning.* Routledge, New York, NY.

22. Nesse, R.M. and Lloyd, A.T. (1992) "The Evolution of Psychodynamic Mechanisms." In *Keywords in Evolutionary Biology,* pp. 601-626.

23. Tudge, C. (2000) *The Impact of the Gene.* Hill and Wang, New York,   NY.

24. Kitcher, P. (1996) *The Lives to Come: The Genetic Revolution and   Human Possibilities.* Simon & Schuster, New York, NY.

Le Doux, J. (2002) *Synaptic Self: How Our Brains Become Who We Are.*   Penguin Books, New York, NY.

25. Ehin, C. (1998) "Fostering Both Sides of Human Nature—The   Foundation For Collaborative Relationships," *Business Horizons,* May- June, pp. 15-25.

26. Toomby, J. and Cosmides, L. (1992) "The Psychological Foundations of   Culture." In *Keywords in Evolutionary Biology,* pp. 3-117. Harvard   University Press, Cambridge, MA.

Zimmer, C. (2004) "Whose Life Would You Save," *Discover*, April, pp.   60-65.

27. Morris, H.J. (2001) "Happiness Explained," *U.S. News & World Report*,   September 3, pp. 46-54.

28. Howard, P.J. (2000) *The Owner's Manual for the Brain.* Brad Press, Austin, TX.

29. Pinker, S. (2003) "Are Your Genes to Blame?" *Time*, January 20, pp. 98-100.

30. Diamond, J. (1999) *Guns, Germs, and Steel.* W.W. Norton & Company,   New York, NY.

Fagan, B.M. (1990) *The Journey from Eden.* Thames and Hudson, New   York, NY.

31. Florida, R. (2004) "No Monopoly on Creativity" in "Breakthrough Ideas   for 2004." *Harvard Business Review*, February, pp. 13-37.

CHAPTER 4

1. Roethlisberger, F.J. and Dickson, W.J. (1939) *Management and the Worker.* Harvard University Press, Cambridge, MA.

2. Edelman, G.M. (1992) *Bright Air, Brilliant Fire.* Basic Books, Harper   Collins, New York, NY.

Kelso, J.A.S. (1995) *Dynamic Patterns: The Self-Organization of Brain and Behavior.* Bradford Books, MIT Press, Cambridge, MA.

Ridley, M. (1999) *Genome.* Harper Collins Publishers, New York, NY.

Wilson, E.O. (1998) *Consilience: The Unity of Knowledge.* Knopf, New York, NY.

3. Kelly, K. (1994) *Out of Control: The Rise of Neo-biological Civilization.*   William Patrick Books, Addison-Wesley, New York, NY.

4. Baumeister, R.F. (1999) *Evil: Inside Human Violence and Cruelty.* W. H. Freeman and Company, New York, NY.

5. Boon, L.E. and Bowen, D.D. (1987) *The Great Writings in Management   and Organizational Behavior.* Random House, New York, NY.

George, C.S. (1972) *The History of Management Thought.* Prentice-Hall, Englewood Cliffs, NJ.

6. Stevens, A. and Price, T. (1996) *.Evolutionary Psychiatry: A New   Beginning.* Routledge, New York, NY.

7. Adler, P.S. and Seok-Woo, K. (2002) "Social Capital: Prospects for a   New Concept," *The Academy of Management Review,* Vol. 27, Nr. 1, pp. 17-40.

8. Nahapiet, J. and Ghoshal, S. (1998) "Social Capital, Intellectual Capital,   and the Organizational Advantage," *The Academy of Management Review,* March, pp. 242-266.

Manville, B. and Ober, J. (2003) "Beyond Empowerment: Building a Company of Citizens," *Harvard Business Review*, January, pp. 48-53.

9. Smith, L. (2001) "The Concept of Intellectual Capital in Mergers and   Acquisitions,"
    Unpublished MBA research paper at Westminster   College of Salt Lake City, UT.,
    Spring.
10. Stauffer, D. (2000) *Nothing but Net.* Capstone, Milford, CT.

CHAPTER 5

1. Watts, D. J. (2003) *Six Degrees.* W. W. Norton & Company, Inc., New   York, NY.
2. Buckingham, M. and Clifton, D.O. (2001) *Now, Discover Your   Strengths.* The Free
    Press, NY.
3. Beersma, B. and coauthors (2003) "Cooperation, Competition, and Team   Performance:
    Towards a Contingency Approach," *The Academy of   Management Journal,* Vol. 46,
    Nr. 5, October, pp. 572-590.
4. Smith, C. and Comer, D. (1994) "Self-Organization in Small Groups,"   *Human
    Relations,*   Vol. 47, No. 5.
5. Gleick, J. (1988) *Chaos: Making a New Science.* Penguin Books, New   York, NY.
    Waldrop, M.M. (1992) *Complexity.* Simon & Schuster, New York, NY.
6. Fletcher, J.K. (1996) "A Relational Approach to the Protean Worker." In   *The Career Is
    Dead—Long Live the Career,* edited by Douglas T. Hall   and Associates, pp. 115-
    124. Jossey-Bass, San Francisco, CA.
    McDonald, M. (2003) "The Mentor Gap," *U. S. News & World Report,*   November
    3, pp. 36-38.
7. Watts, D. J. (2003) *Six Degrees.* W. W. Norton & Company, Inc., New   York, NY.
8. Jassawalla, A.R. and Sashittal, H.C. (2002) "Cultures that Support   Product-Innovation
    Processes." *Academy of Management Executive,*   Vol. 16, No. 3.
9. Gore, V. (1980) "policies," W.L. Gore & Associates internal   memorandum, November
    19, pp. 2-3.
    Gore, W.L. (Undated) *Freedom to Dream.* Unpublished manuscript.

CHAPTER 6

1. Pierce, J.L. and Newstrom, J.W. (2000) *Leaders and the Leadership Process.* Irwin
    McGraw-Hill, New York, NY.
    Weiss, J.W. (2001) *Organizational Behavior and Change.* South-Western   College
    Publishing, Cincinnati, OH.
    Sternberg, R.J. (2003) "WICS: A Model of Leadership in Organizations,"   *Academy
    of   Management Learning & Education,* December, Vol. 2, No. 4, pp. 386-401.
    Bennis, W. B. (2004) "The Seven Ages of the Leader," *Harvard Business Review,*
    January, pp. 46-53.
    Joni, S. (2004) "The Geography of Trust." *Harvard Business Review,*

March, pp. 83-88.

2. Diamond, J. (1999) *Guns, Germs, and Steel.* W.W. Norton & Company,   New York, NY.

    Ehin, C. (1993) "A High-Performance Team Is Not a Multi-Part Machine," *The Journal for Quality and Participation,* December, pp. 38-48.

    Yellen, J.E. (1990) "The Transformation of the Kalahari Kung," *Scientific American,* April, pp. 99-105.

3. George, C.S. (1972) *The History of Management Thought.* Prentice-Hall,   Englewood Cliffs, NJ.

4. Boon, L.E. and Bowen, D.D. (1987) *The Great Writings in Management and Organizational Behavior.* Random House, New York, NY.

5. Pierce, J.L. and Newstrom, J.W. (2000) *Leaders and the Leadership Process.* Irwin McGraw-Hill, New York, NY.

    Weiss, J.W. (2001) *Organizational Behavior and Change.* South-Western   College Publishing, Cincinnati, OH.

6. Ehin, C. (1995) "The Ultimate Advantage of Self-Organizing Systems,"   *The Journal for Quality and Participation,* September, pp. 30-38.

7. Block, P. (1993) *Stewardship: Choosing Service over Self-Interest.*   Berrett-Koehler, San Francisco, CA.

    Collins, J. (2001) *Good to Great.* Harper Business, New York, N.J.

    Golman, D., Boyatzis, R. and McKee (2001) "Primal Leadership: The Hidden Driver of Great Performance," *Harvard Business Review,* December, pp. 42-51.

    Senge, P. (1990) "The Leader's New Work: Building Learning Organizations," *Sloan Management Review,* Fall, pp. 7-23.

8. Bedeian, A. G. (2002) "The Dean's Disease: How the Dark Side of   Power Manifests Itself in the Office of Dean," *Academy of   Management Learning & Education,* Vol. 1,   Nr. 2, December, pp. 164-173.

    Kramer, R. M. (2003) "The Harder They Fall," *Harvard Business Review,*   October, pp. 58-66.

9. Harari, O. (2002) "Open Doors," *Modern Maturity,* January/February,   pp. 48-50.

10. Petzinger, T., Jr. (1999) *The New Pioneers.* Simon & Schuster, New   York, NY.

CHAPTER 7

1. Ashby, W.R. (1956) *An Introduction to Cybernetics.* Chapman and Hall,   London, England.

2. Le Doux, J. (2002) *Synaptic Self: How Our Brains Become Who We Are.*   Penguin Books, New York, NY.

3. Prahalad, C.K. and Hamel, G. (1990) "The Core Competence of the Corporation," *Harvard Business Review,* May-June, pp. 79-91.

4. Mascarenhas, B., Baveja, A. and Jamil, M. (1998) "Dynamic Core   Competencies in Leading Multinational Companies," *California   Management Review*, Vol. 40, No. 4, Summer, pp. 117-132.

5. Wheatley, M.J. (1992) *Leadership and the New Science: Learning About Organization from an Orderly Universe*. Berrett-Koehler, San   Francisco, CA.

6. Edelman, G.M. (1992) *Bright Air, Brilliant Fire*. Basic Books, Harper   Collins, New York, NY.

7. Simon, H.A. (1965) *The Shape of Automation for Men and Management*.   Harper Torchbooks, The Academy Library, New York, NY.

8. Schoderbek, P.P., Schoderbek, C.G. and Kefalas, A.G. (1990)   *Management Systems*. Richard D. Irwin, Inc., Boston, MA.

    Kaplan, R. S. and Norton, (2004) "Measuring the Strategic Readiness of Intangible Assets." *Harvard Business Review*, February, pp. 52-63.

9. McGarvey, R. (1996) "Tomorrow Land," *Entrepreneur*, February, pp.   135-138.

10. Stewart, T. A. (2002) "How to Think With Your Gut," *Business 2.0*, November, pp.   98-104.

11. Gosling, J. and Mintzberg, H. (2003) "The Five Minds of a manager,"   *Harvard Business   Review*, November, pp. 54-63.

12. Senge, P. (1990) *The Fifth Discipline*. Doubleday Currency, New York,   NY.

13. Gross, B. (1998) "The New Math of Ownership," *Harvard Business Review*, November-December, pp. 68-74.

    Rousseau, D. M. and Shperling, Z. (2003) "Piece of the Action: Ownership and the Changing Employment Relationship," *The Academy of Management Review*, Vol. 28, Nr. 4, October.

14. Kelly, K. (1994) *Out of Control: The Rise of Neo-biological Civilization*. William Patrick Books, Addison-Wesley, New York, NY.

CHAPTER 8

1. Ghoshal, S. and Tsai, W. (1998) "Social Capital and Value Creation: The   Role of Intrafirm Networks," *The Academy of Management Journal*,   Vol. 41, No. 4, August, pp. 464-476.

2. Ehin, C. (2000) *Unleashing Intellectual Capital*, Butterworth- Heinemann, Boston, MA.

3. Standfield, K. (2002) *Intangible Management*. Academic Press, San Diego, CA.

4. Schoderbek, P.P., Schoderbek, C.G. and Kefalas, A.G. (1990)   *Management Systems*. Richard D. Irwin, Inc., Boston, MA.

5. Restak, R. (2002) "All in Your Head," *Modern Maturity*   January/February, pp. 58-63.

6. Weiss, J.W. (2001) *Organizational Behavior and Change*. South- Western College Publishing, Cincinnati, OH.

7. Florida, R. (2002) *The Rise of the Creative Class*. Basic Books, New   York, NY.

8. Drucker, P.F. (1999) "Beyond the Information Revolution," *The Atlantic   Monthly,* October, pp. 47-57.

9. Iansiti, M. and Levien, R. (2004) "Strategy as Ecology." *Harvard   Business Review,* March, pp. 68-78.

EPILOGUE

"Genetic Research Goes Swimmingly," (2002) *National Geographic,* January, p .viii.

REFERENCES

Adler, P.S. and Seok-Woo, K. (2002) "Social Capital: Prospects for a New Concept,"
   The Academy of Management Review, Vol. 27, Nr. 1, pp. 17-40.

Allman, J.M. (1999) *Evolving Brains.* Scientific American Library, New York, NY.

Allman, J. and Brothers, L. (1994) "Faces, Fears and Amygdala," *Nature,* December 15,
   pp. 613-614.

Angela, A. and Angela, P. (1993) The Extraordinary Story of Human Origins.
   Prometheus Books, Buffalo, NY.

Ashby, W.R. (1956) *An Introduction to Cybernetics.* Chapman and Hall, London,
   England.

Axelrod, R. (1984) *The Evolution of Cooperation,* Basic Books, Inc., New York, NY.

Baily, K. (1987) *Human Paleopsychology: Applications to Aggression and Pathological
   Processes.* Lawrence Erlbaum, Hove and London, Hillsdale, NJ.

Bakan, D. (1966) *The Duality of Human Existence.* Beacon Books, Boston, MA.

Barash, D.P. and Barash, I.L. (2000) *The Mammal in the Mirror.* W.H. Freeman and
   Company, New York, NY.

Barkow, J.H., Cosmides, L. and Toomby, J. (1995) *The Adapted Mind: Evolutionary
   Psychology and the Generation of Culture.* Oxford University Press,
   New York, NY.

Barlow, C., ed. (1994) *Evolution Extended: Biological Debates on the Meaning of Life.*
   MIT Press, Cambridge, MA.

Baumeister, R.F. (1999) *Evil: Inside Human Violence and Cruelty.* W. H. Freeman and
   Company, New York, NY.

Bedeian, A. G. (2002) "The Dean's Disease: How the Dark Side of Power Manifests
   Itself in the Office of Dean," *Academy of Management Learning & Education,*
   Vol. 1, Nr. 2, December, pp. 164-173.

Beersma, B. and coauthors (2003) "Cooperation, Competition, and Team Performance:
   Towards a Contingency Approach," *The Academy of Management Journal*, Vol. 46,
   Nr. 5, October, pp. 572-590.

Bennis, W. B. (2004) "The Seven Ages of the Leader," *Harvard Business Review*, January, pp. 46-53.

Block, P. (1993) Stewardship: *Choosing Service Over Self-Interest*. Berrett-Koehler, San Francisco, CA.

Bolino, M. C. and Turnley, W. H. (2003) "Going the Extra Mile: Cultivating and Managing Employee Citizenship Behavior," Academy of Management Executive, Vol. 17, Nr. 3, August, pp. 60-71.

Boon, L.E. and Bowen, D.D. (1987) *The Great Writings in Management and Organizational Behavior*. Random House, New York, NY.

Bouchard, T.J. (1994) "Genes, Environment and Personality," *Science*, Vol. 264, pp. 1700-1701.

Buckingham, M. and Clifton, D.O. (2001) *Now, Discover Your Strengths*. The Free Press, New York, NY.

Case, J. (1997) "Opening the Books," *Harvard Business Review*, March-April, pp. 118-127.

Chance, M.R.A. (1988) "Introduction," in *Social Fabrics of the Mind*, edited by M.R.A. Chance. Lawrence Erlbaum, Hove and London, Hillsdale, NJ.

Cohen, W.M. and Levinthal, D.A. (1990) "A New Perspective on Learning and Innovation," *Administrative Science Quarterly*, Vol. 35, pp. 128- 152.

Collins, T.C. and Porras, T.I. (1994) *Built to Last: Successful Habits of Visionary Companies*. Harper Collins, New York, NY.

Collins, J. (2001) *Good to Great*. Harper Business, New York, N.J.

Colt, G.H. (1998) "Were You Born That Way?" *Life*, April, pp.39-49.

Colvin, G. (1997) "The Changing Act of Becoming Unbeatable," *Fortune*, November 24, pp. 299-300.

Cross, R. and Prusak, L. (2002) "The People Who Make Organizations Go—or Stop," *Harvard Business Review*, June 2002, pp. 105-112.

Darwin, C. (1936) *The Origin of Species and the Descent of Man*. The Modern Library, New York, NY.

Davis, T.R.V. (1997) "Open-Book Management: Its Promise and Pitfalls," *Organizational Dynamics*, Winter, pp. 7-20.

Deacon, T.W. (1997) *The Symbolic Species*. W.W. Norton & Company, New York, NY.

DeLong, D.W. and Fahey, L. "Diagnosing Cultural Barriers to Knowledge Management," *Academy of Management Executive*, November, pp. 113-127.

Dennett, D.C. (1995) *Darwin's Dangerous Idea*. Touchstone (Simon & Schuster Inc.), New York, NY.

Diamond, J. (1992) *The Third Chimpanzee*. Harper Collins Publishers, New York, NY.

Diamond, J. (1999) *Guns, Germs, and Steel*. W.W. Norton & Company, New York, NY.

Dunbar, R. (1996) *Grooming, Gossip, and the Evaluation of Language*. Harvard University Press, Cambridge, MA.

Drucker, P.F. (1999) "Beyond the Information Revolution," *The Atlantic Monthly*, October, pp. 47-57.

Druskat, V.U. and Wolff, S.B. (2001) "Building the Emotional Intelligence of Groups," *Harvard Business Review,* March, pp. 81-90.

Edelman, G.M. (1992) *Bright Air, Brilliant Fire.* Basic Books, HarperCollins, New York, NY.

Ehin, C. (2000) *Unleashing Intellectual Capital,* Butterworth-Heinemann, Boston, MA.

Ehin, C. (1998) "Fostering Both Sides of Human Nature—The Foundation For Collaborative Relationships," *Business Horizons,* May-June, pp. 15-25.

Ehin, C. (1995) "The Quest for Empowering Organizations: Some Lessons From Our Foraging Past," *Organization Science,* November-December, pp. 666-671.

Ehin, C. (1995) "The Ultimate Advantage of Self-Organizing Systems," *The Journal for Quality and Participation,* September, pp. 30-38.

Ehin, C. (1993) "A High-Performance Team Is Not a Multi-Part Machine," *The Journal for Quality and Participation,* December, pp. 38-48.

Eldredge, N. and Gould, S.J. (1972) "Punctuated Equilibria: An Alternative To Phyletic Gradualism." In *Models of Paleobiology,* edited by T.J.M. Schopf, pp. 82-115. Freeman, Cooper and Co., San Francisco, CA.

Emery, M., ed. (1993) *Participative Design for Participative Democracy.* Australia National University, Canberra, Australia.

Fagan, B.M. (1990) *The Journey from Eden.* Thames and Hudson, New York, NY.

Fletcher, J.K. (1996) "A Relational Approach to the Protean Worker." In *The Career Is Dead—Long Live the Career,* edited by Douglas T. Hall and Associates, pp. 115-124. Jossey-Bass, San Francisco, CA.

Florida, R. (2004) "No Monopoly on Creativity" in "Breakthrough Ideas for 2004." *Harvard Business Review,* February, pp. 13-37.

Florida, R. (2002) *The Rise of the Creative Class.* Basic Books, New York, NY.

Fortey, R. (1997) *Life.* Knopf, New York, NY.

Fox, R. (1989) *The Search for Society: Quest for a Biosocial Science and Morality.* Rutgers University Press, New Brunswick, NJ.

Fulmer, R.M., Gibbs, P. and Keys, J.D. (1998) "The Second Generation Learning Organization: New Tools for Sustaining Competitive Advantage," *Organizational Dynamics,* Autumn, pp. 7-20.

"Future Visions," (2003) *Time,* February 17, pp. 60-61.

"Genetic Research Goes Swimmingly," (2002) *National Geographic,* January, p. viii.

George, C.S. (1972) *The History of Management Thought.* Prentice-Hall, Englewood Cliffs, NJ.

Ghoshal, S. and Tsai, W. (1998) "Social Capital and Value Creation: The Role of Intrafirm Networks," *The Academy of Management Journal,* Vol. 41, No. 4, August, pp. 464-476.

Gleick, J. (1988) *Chaos: Making a New Science.* Penguin Books, New York, NY.

Goffee, R. and Jones, G. (2000) "Why Should Anyone Be Led by You?" *Harvard Business Review,* September-October, pp. 63-70.

Golman, D., Boyatzis, R. and McKee (2001) "Primal Leadership: The Hidden Driver of

Great Performance," *Harvard Business Review,* December, pp. 42-51.

Gore, R. (1997) "Tracking the First of Our Kind," *National Geographic,* Vol. 192, No. 3, pp. 92-99.

Gore, R. (1997) "The Dawn of Humans," *National Geographic,* Vol. 192, No. 1, pp. 96-113.

Gosling, J. and Mintzberg, H. (2003) "The Five Minds of a manager," *Harvard Business Review,* November, pp. 54-63.

Gould, S.J. (1996) *Full House.* Harmony Books, New York, NY.

Gould, S.J. (1993) *Eight Little Piggies: Reflections in Natural History.* Norton, New York, NY.

Gross, B. (1998) "The New Math of Ownership," *Harvard Business Review,* November-December, pp. 68-74.

Haken, H. (1981) *The Science of Structure: Synergetics.* Van Nostrand Reinhold, NewYork, NY.

Halal, W.E., ed. (1998) *The Infinite Resource: Creating and Leading Knowledge Enterprises.* Jossey-Bass, San Francisco, CA.

Hallowell, E.M. (1999) "The Human Moment at Work," *Harvard Business Review,* January-February, pp. 58-66.

Hamel, G. and Välikangas, L. (2003) "The Quest for Resilience," *Harvard Business Review,* September, pp. 52-63.

Hansen, T.M., Nohria, N. and Tierney, T. (1999) "What's Your Strategy for Managing Knowledge?" *Harvard Business Review,* March-April, pp. 106-116.

Harari, O. (2002) "Open Doors", *Modern Maturity,* January/February, pp. 48-50.

Harris, M. (1989) "Life Without Chiefs," *New Age Journal,* November-December, pp. 42-45.

Herbert, W. (1997) "Politics of Biology," *U.S. News & World Report,* April 21, pp. 72-80.

Herzberg, F. (1987) "One More Time: How Do You Motivate Employees?" *Harvard Business Review,* September-October, pp. 109-120.

Hitt, M.A., Keats, B.W. and DeMarie, S.M. (1998) "Navigating in the New Competitive Landscape: Building Strategic Flexibility and Competitive Advantage in the 21st Century," *Academy of Management Executives,* November, pp. 22-43.

Hoecklin, L. (1995) *Managing Cultural Differences.* Addison-Wesley, New York, NY.

Howard, P.J. (2000) *The Owner's Manual for The Brain.* Brad Press, Austin, TX.

Iansiti, M. and Levien, R. (2004) "Strategy as Ecology." *Harvard Business Review,* March, pp. 68-78.

Jassawalla, A.R. and Sashittal, H.C. (2002) "Cultures that Support Product-Innovation Processes." *Academy of Management Executive,* Vol. 16, No. 3.

Johanson, D. and Johanson, L. (1994) *Ancestors: In Search of Human Origins.* Willard Books, New York, NY.

Joni, S. (2004) "The Geography of Trust." *Harvard Business Review,* March, pp. 83-88.

Kaplan, R. S. and Norton, (2004) "Measuring the Strategic Readiness of Intangible

Assets." *Harvard Business Review, February*, pp. 52-63.

Kauffman, S. (1995) *At Home in the Universe.* Oxford University Press, New York, NY.

Kayes, D. C. (2002) "Experiential Learning and Its Critics: Preserving the Role of Experience in Management Learning and Education," *Academy of Management Learning & Education*, Vol. 1, Nr. 2, December, pp. 137- 149.

Keidel, R.W. (1994) "Rethinking Organizational Design," *Academy of Management Executives*, Vol. 8, No. 4, pp. 12-20.

Keller, E.F. and Lloyd, E.A., eds. (1992) *Keywords in Evolutionary Biology.* Harvard University Press, Cambridge, MA.

Kelly, K. (1998) *New Rules for The New Economy.* Viking, New York, NY.

Kelly, K. (1994) *Out of Control: The Rise of Neo-biological Civilization.* William Patrick Books, Addison-Wesley, New York, NY.

Kelso, J.A.S. (1995) *Dynamic Patterns: The Self-Organization of Brain and Behavior.* Bradford Books, MIT Press, Cambridge, MA.

Kets De Vries, M.F.R. (1999) "High-Performance Teams: Lessons from the Pygmies," *Organizational Dynamics*, Winter, pp. 66-77.

Kiernan, M.J. (1993) "The New Strategic Architecture: Learning to Compete in the Twenty-first Century," *Academy of Management Executives*, Vol. 7, No. 1, pp. 7-21.

Kim, C. and Mauborgne, R. (1997) "Fair Process: Managing in the Knowledge Economy," *Harvard Business Review*, July-August, pp. 65-75.

Kitcher, P. (1996) *The Lives to Come: The Genetic Revolution and Human Possibilities.* Simon & Schuster, New York, NY.

Kofman, F. and Senge, P.M. (1993) "Communities of Learning: The Heart Of Learning Organizations," *Organizational Dynamics*, Fall, pp. 5-23.

Kohn, A. (1998) "How Incentives Undermine Performance," *The Journal For Quality and Participation*, March-April, pp. 7-13.

Kohn, A. (1992) *No Contest: The Case Against Competition.* Houghton Mifflin, New York, NY.

Kramer, R. M. (2003) "The Harder They Fall," Harvard Business Review, October, pp. 58-66.

Leakey, R. and Lewin, R. (1995) *The Sixth Extinction: Patterns of Life and the Future of Humankind.* Doubleday, New York, NY.

Leakey, R. and Lewin, R. (1992) *Origins Reconsidered: In Search of What Makes Us Human.* Doubleday, New York, NY.

Le Doux, J. (2002) *Synaptic Self: How Our Brains Become Who We Are.* Penguin Books, New York, NY.

Lee, R.B. (1979) *The !Kung San: Men, Women and Work in a Foraging Society.* Cambridge University Press, London, England.

Leonard-Barton, D. (1995) *Wellsprings of Knowledge: Building and Sustaining the Sources of Innovation.* Harvard Business School press, Boston, MA.

Lengnick-Hall, M.L. and Lengnick-Hall, C.A. (2003) "HR's Role in Building Relationship Networks," *Academy of Management Executive*, Vol. 17, No. 4, pp. 54-63.

Linden, E. (1992) "A Curious Kinship: Apes and Humans," *National Geographic,*
Vol. 189, No. 1, pp. 2-45.

MacLean, P.D. (1973) *A Triune Concept of the Brain Behavior.* University of Toronto
Press, Toronto, Canada.

Mann, C.C. (1994) "Behavioral Genetics in Transition," *Science,* Vol. 264,
pp. 1686-1689.

Manville, B. and Ober, J. (2003) "Beyond Empowerment: Building a Company of
Citizens," *Harvard Business Review,* January, pp. 48-53.

Marshall, L. (1976) *The! Kung of Nyae Nyae.* Harvard University Press, Cambridge, MA.

Mascarenhas, B., Baveja, A. and Jamil, M. (1998) "Dynamic Core Competencies in
Leading Multinational Companies," *California Management Review,* Vol. 40,
No. 4, Summer, pp. 117-132.

Mayer, E. (2001) *What Evolution Is.* Basic Books, New York, NY.

McDonald, M. (2003) "The Mentor Gap," *U. S. News & World Report,* November 3,
pp. 36-38.

McGregor, D. M. (1960) *The Human Side of Enterprise.* McGraw-Hill, New York, NY.

McGarvey, R. (1996) "Tomorrow Land," *Entrepreneur,* February, pp. 135-138.

Monastersky, R. (1998) "The Rise of Life on Earth," *National Geographic,* March,
pp. 54-81.

Morris, H.J. (2001) "Happiness Explained," *U.S. News & World Report,* September 3,
pp. 46-54.

Nahapiet, J. and Ghoshal, S. (1998) "Social Capital, Intellectual Capital, and The
Organizational Advantage," *The Academy of Management Review,* March,
pp. 242-266.

Nesse, R.M. and Lloyd, A.T. (1992) "The Evolution of Psychodynamic Mechanisms."
In *Keywords in Evolutionary Biology,* pp. 601-626.

Nicholson, N. (1997) "Evolutionary Psychology: Toward a New View of Human Nature
and Organizational Society," *Human Relations,* Vol. 50, No. 9, pp. 1053-1078.

Ornstein, R. (1986) *Multimind.* Mifflin, Boston, MA.

Pasternak, C. A. (2003) Quest: The Essence of Humanity. John Wiley & Sons Ltd.,
West Sussex, England.

Petzinger, T., Jr. (1999) *The New Pioneers.* Simon & Schuster, New York, NY.

Petzinger, T., Jr. (1997) "Self-Organization Will Free Employees to Act Like Bosses,"
Wall Street Journal, January 3, p. 31.

Pfeffer, T. and Veiga, T.F. (1999) "Putting People First for Organizational Success,"
Academy of Management Executives, Vol. 13, No. 2, May, pp. 37-48.

Pierce, J.L. and Newstrom, J.W. (2000) *Leaders and the Leadership Process.*
Irwin McGraw-Hill, New York, NY.

Pinker, S. (1997) *How the Mind Works.* W. W. Norton & Company, New York, NY.

Pinker, S. (2002) *The Blank Slate: The Modern Denial of Human Nature.*
Viking Penguin, New York, NY.

Pinker, S. (2003) "Are Your Genes to Blame?" Time, January 20, pp. 98-100.

Polanyi, M. (1958) *Personal Knowledge: Towards a Post-Critical Philosophy.* University of Chicago Press, Chicago, IL.

Pollack, R. (1994) *Signs of Life: The Language and Meaning of DNA.* Houghton Mifflin, New York, NY.

Power, M. (1991) *The Egalitarians—Human and Chimpanzee.* Cambridge University Press, New York, NY.

Prahalad, C.K. and Hamel, G. (1990) "The Core Competence of the Corporation," *Harvard Business Review,* May-June, pp. 79-91.

Raup, D.M. (1991) *Extinction: Bad Genes or Bad Luck?* Norton, New York, NY.

Restak, R. (1984) *The Brain.* Bantam Books, New York, NY.

Restak, R. (2002) "All in Your Head," *Modern Maturity,* January/February, pp. 58-63.

Ridley, M. (1999) *Genome.* Harper Collins Publishers, New York, NY.

Robbins, S. P. (2002) *The Truth About Managing People.* Financial Times. Prentice Hall, New York, NY.

Robbins, H. and Finnley, M. (1995) *Why Teams Don't Work.* Peterson's Pacesetter Books, Princeton, NJ.

Roethlisberger, F.J. and Dickson, W.J. (1939) *Management and the Worker.* Harvard University Press, Cambridge, MA.

Rousseau, D. M. and Shperling, Z. (2003) "Piece of the Action: Ownership and the Changing Employment Relationship," *The Academy of Management Review,* Vol. 28, Nr. 4, October.

Rubin, H. (1999) "Only the Pronoid Survive," *Fast Company,* November.

Sagan, C. (1977) *The Dragons of Eden.* Random House, New York, NY.

Scanlan, B.K. (1981)"Creating a Climate for Achievement," *Business Horizons,* March-April, pp. 5-9.

Schoderbek, P.P., Schoderbek, C.G. and Kefalas, A.G. (1990) *Management Systems.* Richard D. Irwin, Inc., Boston, MA.

Schrof, J. (1997) "What Is a Memory Made of?" *U.S. News & World Report,* August 25.

Senge, P. (1990) *The Fifth Discipline.* Doubleday Currency, New York, NY.

Senge, P. (1990) "The Leader's New Work: Building Learning Organizations," *Sloan Management Review,* Fall, pp. 7-23.

Shirky, C. (2004) "Watching the Patterns Emerge" in "Breakthrough Ideas for 2004." *Harvard Business Review,* February, pp. 13-37.

Shreeve, J. (1999) "Secrets of the Gene," *National Geographic,* October, pp. 42-75.

Shute, N. (2001) "Where We Come From," *U.S. World & News Report,* January 29, pp. 34-41.

Simon, H.A. (1965) *The Shape of Automation for Men and Management.* Harper Torchbooks, The Academy Library, New York, NY.

Smith, C. and Comer, D. (1994) "Self-Organization in Small Groups," *Human Relations,* Vol. 47, No. 5.

Smith, L. (2001) "The Concept of Intellectual Capital in Mergers and Acquisitions,"

Unpublished MBA research paper at Westminster College of Salt Lake City, UT, Spring.

Spreitzer, G. (1996) "Social Structural Characteristics of Psychologic Empowerment," *Academy of Management Journal,* April, Vol. 39(2), pp. 485-504.

Standfield, K. (2002) *Intangible Management.* Academic Press, San Diego, CA.

Stanford, C. (2001) *Significant Others: The Ape-Human Continuum and the Quest for Human Nature.* Basic Books, New York, NY.

Stauffer, D. (2000) *Nothing but Net.* Capstone, Milford, CT.

Sternberg, R.J. (2003) "WICS: A Model of Leadership in Organizations," *Academy of Management Learning & Education,* December, Vol. 2, No. 4, pp. 386-401.

Stevens, A. and Price, T. (1996) *Evolutionary Psychiatry: A New Beginning.* Routledge, New York, NY.

Stewart, T.A. (1997) *Intellectual Capital: The New Wealth of Organizations.* Doubleday/Currency, New York, NY.

Stewart, T. A. (2002) "How to Think With Your Gut," *Business 2.0,* November, pp. 98-104.

Sveiby, K.E. (1997) *The New Organizational Wealth: Managing & Measuring Knowledge-Based Assets.* Berrett-Koehler, San Francisco, CA.

Toomby, J. and Cosmides, L. (1992) "The Psychological Foundations of Culture." In *Keywords in Evolutionary Biology,* pp. 3-117. Harvard University Press, Cambridge, MA.

Tudge, C. (2000) *The Impact of the Gene.* Hill and Wang, New York, NY.

Wageman, R. (1997) "Critical Success Factors for Creating Superb Self-Managing Teams," *Organizational Dynamics,* Summer, pp. 49-61.

Waldrop, M.M. (1992) *Complexity.* Simon & Schuster, New York, NY.

Watts, D. J. (2003) *Six Degrees.* W. W. Norton & Company, Inc., New York, NY.

Weiss, J.W. (2001) *Organizational Behavior and Change.* South-Western College Publishing, Cincinnati, OH.

Wheatley, M.J. (1992) *Leadership and the New Science: Learning About Organization from an Orderly Universe.* Berrett-Koehler, San Francisco, CA.

Williams, G. (1966) *Adaption and Natural Selection.* Princeton University Press, Princeton, NJ.

Wilson, E.O. (1998) *Consilience: The Unity of Knowledge.* Knopf, New York, NY.

Yellen, J.E. (1990) "The Transformation of the Kalahari Kung," *Scientific American,* April, pp. 99-105.

Zahra, S.A. and George, G. (2002) "Absorptive Capacity: A Review, Reconceptualization, and Extension," *The Academy of Management Review,* April, Vol. 27 (2), pp. 185-203.

Zimmer, C. (2003) "Great Mysteries of Human Evolution," *Discover,* September, pp. 33-43.

Zimmer, C. (2004) "Whose Life Would You Save," *Discover,* April, pp. 60-65.

INDEX